WITH JESUS TO THE CROSS

A Lenten Guide on the Sunday Mass Readings:

Year C

A Catholic Guide for Small Groups

the
evangelical
catholic

forming disciples.
training leaders.

theWORD
among us®
press

Published by The Word Among Us Press
7115 Guilford Drive, Suite 100
Frederick, Maryland 21704
www.wau.org

20 19 18 17 16   2 3 4 5 6

Nihil obstat: The Reverend Michael Morgan, J.D., J.C.L.
                 Censor Librorum
                 November 30, 2015

Imprimatur: Most Reverend Felipe J. Estevez
                 Bishop of St. Augustine
                 November 30, 2015

ISBN: 978-1-59325-286-1
eISBN:978-1-59325-478-0

Cover design by Andrea Alvarez
Cover image: *Compassion I*. 1897.
William-Adolphe Bouguereau (1825-1905)
Location: Musee d'Orsay, Paris, France
Photo Credit: © RMN-Grand Palais/Art Resource, NY

Made and printed in the United States of America

Library of Congress Control Number: 2015958263

Contents

Introduction

> "Even now," **says the LORD,**
> "return to me with **all your heart.**"
>
> Joel 2:12
>
> (from Ash Wednesday readings)

When we care about something or someone with our whole hearts, we never find it difficult to engage. We throw ourselves into what we care about passionately.

The athlete dedicates himself to daily rigorous training to compete at his peak. The music student spends untold hours practicing her instrument to perform exquisitely at the concert. Parents care for their children with devotion because they love nothing in the world more than these small precious people. We see this kind of wholehearted dedication every day of our lives.

Sometimes we see it toward God.

That is how we hope you will approach this study: with the dedication that comes only from becoming wholehearted about your relationship with God.

This takes a special kind of commitment. God can seem remote, and faith, a matter for the far-off future, insufficiently immediate to demand our attention. It is easy to think we cannot possibly bring the intensity of interest and engagement to God that we bring to our relationships, our studies, our passions, our goals and aspirations. Only saints and fanatics do that.

But God doesn't say, "I want only holy people to return to me." He calls every one of us to come to him with our whole hearts.

If you were to be seriously injured in a car wreck this very night, what do you think would matter more—God or your goals and aspirations? Through Lent, the Church says, "Don't wait until the catastrophe. Realize *now* that your hope is in a God who has 'come to deliver' us" (see Week 3; Exodus 3:8).

God doesn't want a relationship with you only when you're in crisis. God loves us just as parents love their children. God wants that relationship *right now*, every day, because that is the way God loves and tends us.

God will not force his way into our hearts. We must invite God. When we realize we want more than anything else for God to make each of us a "new creation" (see Week 4; 2 Corinthians 5:17)—not at some unforeseen future time but right now—we will accept his invitation into a deeper relationship through Jesus. If you give an inch, God will take a mile. God is so in love with you that he can't resist rushing in to heal your heart and make you new.

Inviting God into our lives to transform us through the Lenten readings is what this guide is all about.

Transformation from a mediocre sports player to a true athlete or from a dabbling dilettante to a concert performer only happens if we commit wholeheartedly to the process that it requires. If we want God to transform our lives, then we must give him the time and opportunity to bring us more deeply into the life, death, and resurrection of his Son, Jesus.

The big difference is that God doesn't care about our "performance" in prayer; he just wants to be with us! Making time for that takes commitment on our part.

We know what a halfhearted commitment means: that diet we are "sort of" doing, those books on our nightstand we might read someday, the project we sporadically work on. The gain is minimal—if we gain anything at all—because we haven't committed to it with our whole hearts.

Don't let that happen to you this Lent.

This guide is designed so that you, or your small group if you're in one, can reflect during the preceding week on the Scripture passages that will be read at Mass on the upcoming Sunday. This will allow God to speak to you much more than if you were to hear these passages for the first time during Mass.

Because the first session of *With Jesus to the Cross* discusses the readings for the First Sunday of Lent, your small group will need to meet during the week of Ash Wednesday.

If you aren't in a group, study the Scripture passages and answer the questions for yourself. While a group discussion always broadens our understanding and provides the Christian community we all need, you can still benefit from encountering the Scriptures in advance of Mass and allowing God to guide your thoughts.

Six studies take you through Passion Sunday. Because Holy Week includes liturgical prayers for the three highest holy days of the Church, no additional materials are provided for that week. Attend as many Holy Week services as you can—it will complete your Lenten experience.

Meet again to discuss the Easter Sunday session (Week 7) during the Octave of Easter. (This is the traditional designation of the eight days of the Easter feast, from Easter Sunday to the following Sunday.)

If you faithfully attend this Lenten group and practice the spiritual exercises provided in the "Connection to the Cross This Week" section of each session, God will transform your life in some way. All you need to do is to bring your whole heart. You won't regret it.

How to Use This Small Group Guide

Welcome to *With Jesus to the Cross: Year C*, a small group guide designed to help people know Jesus of Nazareth more deeply and understand more fully the implications of his death and resurrection.

Weekly Sessions

The weekly sessions use the Sunday Mass readings for Lent to help you more deeply enter into the mystery of Christ's life and suffering, and our redemption. Each session includes written opening and closing prayer suggestions, the Scripture passages to be discussed that week, questions for discussion, ideas for action, and prayer prompts to carry you through the week.

The sessions in this guide are self-contained. If you or a friend attends for the first time on Week 3, there won't be a need to "catch up," because anyone can just dive right in with the rest of the group. As with Lent, instead of building sequentially, the sessions deepen thematically, helping you engage more with Jesus and the cross little by little.

The more you take notes, jot down ideas or questions, underline verses in your Bible (if you bring one to your small group— *recommended!*), and refer back to the sessions of previous weeks, the more God has the opportunity to speak to you through the discussion and the ideas he places in your heart. As with anything else, the more you put in, the more you get back.

The best way to take advantage of each week's discussion is to carry the theme into your life by using the "Connection to the

Cross This Week" section. Think of it as a launching pad to meet Jesus every day. The exercises will allow Jesus to enlighten your heart and mind on both the suffering of Lent and the joy of the resurrection. If you're discussing the readings with a small group, the facilitator will give you the chance to share experiences from the previous week, and will talk about the recommendations for the upcoming week during each session.

Each weekly session includes the daily Mass readings for the coming week. You can look these up in your Bible or use several popular free apps that feature the daily readings, such as *Laudate* and *iMissal*. In addition, the daily readings are available at the US Conference of Catholic Bishops' website, usccb.org, which also features an audio version (http://usccb.org/bible/readings-audio.cfm).

You could consider attending daily Mass sometime during Lent, or even weekly, if that's not something you already do. Many spiritual riches come from more frequent reception of the Eucharist.

Appendices

Helpful appendices for both participants and facilitators supplement the weekly materials. Appendices A through E are for participants, and Appendices F through H are for group facilitators.

Prior to your first group meeting, please read Appendix A, "Small Group Discussion Guide." These guidelines will help every person in the group set a respectful tone that creates the space for encountering Christ together.

This small group will differ from other discussion groups you may have experienced. Is it a lecture? No. A book club? No. Appendix A will help you understand what this small group is and how you can help seek a "Spirit-led" discussion. Every member is responsible for the quality of the group dynamics. This appendix will give you helpful tidbits for being a supportive and involved member of the group.

Appendix B is a resource to enhance and deepen your relationship with Jesus. In it you will find a step-by-step guide for reading Scripture on your own. It shows you how to meditate and apply what you find there. Appendix B also offers help in finding other spiritual reading that can enhance and deepen your appreciation for the teachings and person of Jesus.

Appendix C supplements the session for the Second Sunday of Lent, "Listening to God." It provides direction on ways both to hear and talk to God, and includes thoughts from one of the Church's greatest teachers on prayer, St. Teresa of Avila.

Appendix D provides a way to move toward forgiving deep hurts. It supplements the Fourth Sunday of Lent, "Embracing Forgiveness." Forgiveness takes time, and often assistance and guidance as well. This appendix shares the wisdom of a Catholic scholar who has researched the process of forgiveness and how it unfolds.

In Appendix E, you will find a guide to the Sacrament of Reconciliation. Commonly known as "Confession," the Sacrament of Reconciliation bridges the distance between us and God that can be caused by a variety of reasons, including unrepented sin. The Church teaches Catholics to receive this sacrament each Lent, but it is tremendously helpful to practice it more frequently. If you want to grow closer to Jesus and experience great peace, the Sacrament of Reconciliation is an indispensable way to do so. This appendix leads you through the steps of preparing for and going to Confession in order to lessen any anxiety you might feel.

While Appendices A–E are important for small group participants and facilitators alike, Appendices F–H support the facilitator in his or her role.

A facilitator is not a teacher. His or her role is to buoy the conversation, encourage fruitful group discussion, and tend to the group dynamics.

In Appendix F, the group facilitator will find guidance and best practices for facilitating a small group successfully. We've put together recommendations for some possible pesky group dynamics. You will find guidelines on what makes a great group work: building genuine friendships, calling for the Holy Spirit to be the group's true facilitator, and seeking joy together.

Appendix G takes the facilitator from the general to the specific, providing detailed leader notes for each session of *With Jesus to the Cross*. Use this appendix as you prepare for the group meetings on those weeks. The notes give you a "heads up" on the content and issues that pertain to discussion that the facilitator should address.

Appendix H helps the facilitator in leading prayer and encouraging participation in prayer by group members. While the material in each session includes a suggested prayer, Appendix H guides the facilitator in how to pray aloud extemporaneously and help others in the group to do so as well.

Learning this skill is important. It will model for the group members how to talk to Jesus in their own words. Closing with extemporaneous prayers is an extremely valuable way to honor the time you have spent together by offering up the discoveries, questions, and joys of your conversation. Appendix H will help you guide your group from awkward beginnings to a deepening experience of talking to God.

Appendix H also gives the facilitator more information about how to use the "Connection to the Cross This Week" sections in each session. Facilitators should encourage and support group members in their personal engagement with the topics discussed as they deepen their commitment to allow Jesus to become more and more a part of their lives.

Enjoy the adventure!

1st

Sunday of Lent
Hope in the Desert

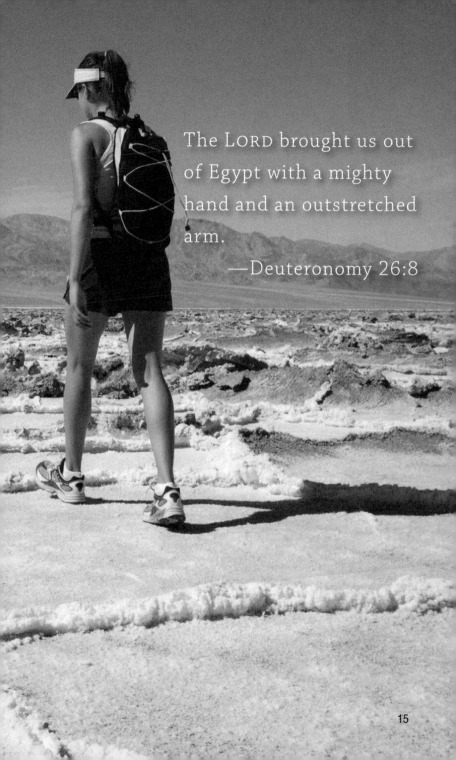

The LORD brought us out of Egypt with a mighty hand and an outstretched arm.

—Deuteronomy 26:8

Ask one person to pray the following prayer aloud slowly.

In the name of the Father, and of the Son, and of the Holy Spirit.

Father, you see us always, and listen to us whenever we pray, even if it is in secret. Hear our prayers now.

Jesus, you said that when two or three gather in your name, you are here among us (Matthew 18:20). We gather now to understand you better and to follow you more closely. Be here among us.

Holy Spirit, you intercede and pray within us when we ourselves do not know how to pray. Let us hear your voice speaking to our hearts through the Scriptures. Guide our discussion and unite us with bonds of love.

Lord God, we trust in your promises. We pause before you now to recollect ourselves, to take a deep breath, and to acknowledge your presence with us.

(Pause)

We thank you for this time we have to spend with you meditating on your word. Please give us the hope we need to trust in your promises.

We ask this through Christ our Lord. **Amen**.

Ask one person to read the following paragraph aloud.

In this First Sunday of Lent, the readings show us God's faithfulness to his promises. We look back to the Israelites' salvation from Egypt and look ahead with hope to the resurrection, God's ultimate promise of salvation. As we begin our own journey into the desert this Lent, the Church reminds us of God's promise to lead us to true freedom.

1. Has a friend or family member ever promised to do something for you? Did he or she follow through? How did their faithfulness to the promise affect your future relationship with this person?

2. Why do you think it is so difficult to trust God when we say that we believe God is all-powerful?

Ask one person to read the Scripture passage aloud.

Deuteronomy 26:4-10

⁴Then the priest shall take the basket from your hand, and set it down before the altar of the LORD your God. ⁵"And you shall make response before the LORD your God, 'A wandering Aramean was my father; and he went down into Egypt and sojourned there, few in number; and there he became a nation, great, mighty, and populous. ⁶And the Egyptians treated us harshly, and afflicted us, and laid upon us hard bondage. ⁷Then we cried to the LORD the God of our fathers, and the LORD heard our voice, and saw our affliction, our toil, and our oppression; ⁸and the LORD brought us out of Egypt with a mighty hand and an outstretched arm, with great terror, with signs and wonders; ⁹and he brought us into this place and gave us this land, a land flowing with milk and honey. ¹⁰And behold, now I bring the first of the fruit of the ground, which thou, O LORD, hast given me.' And you shall set it down before the LORD your God, and worship before the LORD your God."

3. What trials does the author recount in the history of the Israelite people?

4. What characterizes the life of a slave? How might you view God if you were enslaved like the Israelites?

5. What triumphs does the author list?

6. What role did God play in the Israelites' history?

7. When you look back at your life, what trials and triumphs do you see? Can you see God working in those events of your life?

8. The Lord promised his people that he would bring them to the Promised Land flowing with milk and honey. What promises has God made to us in the Scriptures? Do you have hope that God will follow through on these promises?

Ask one person to read the Scripture passage aloud.

Luke 4:1-13

[1]And Jesus, full of the Holy Spirit, returned from the Jordan, and was led by the Spirit [2]for forty days in the wilderness, tempted by the devil. And he ate nothing in those days; and when they were ended, he was hungry. [3]The devil said to him, "If you are the Son of God, command this stone to become bread." [4]And Jesus answered him, "It is written, 'Man shall not live by bread alone.'" [5]And the devil took him up, and showed him all the kingdoms of the world in a moment of time, [6]and said to him, "To you I will give all this authority and their glory; for it has been delivered to me, and I give it to whom I will. [7]If you, then, will worship me, it shall all be yours." [8]And Jesus answered him, "It is written,

> 'You shall worship the LORD your God,
> and him only shall you serve.'"

⁹ And he took him to Jerusalem, and set him on the pinnacle of the temple, and said to him, "If you are the Son of God, throw yourself down from here; ¹⁰ for it is written,

'He will give his angels charge of you, to guard you,'
¹¹ and
'On their hands they will bear you up,
lest you strike your foot against a stone.'"

¹² And Jesus answered him, "It is said, 'You shall not tempt the Lord your God.'" ¹³ And when the devil had ended every temptation, he departed from him until an opportune time.

9. What is Jesus' condition when he encounters the devil?

10. What symbolic significance would the desert have for the Jewish people of Jesus' time? What does the desert call to mind for you?

11. In what three ways does the devil tempt Jesus?

12. How does Jesus resist? What do you think it was like for Jesus to be tempted?

13. What does this interaction show us about Jesus?

14. How are our temptations the same as Jesus' in the desert? How are they different? What hopes must we hold to resist?

15. In what ways can we imitate Jesus' response to the devil?

Jesus was able to resist the devil with the help of Scripture passages he knew so well that they were written on his heart. In his apostolic exhortation *Catechesis in Our Time,* St. John Paul II wrote, "A certain memorization of the words of Jesus, of important Bible passages. . . . is a real need" (55).

Memorizing Scripture is one of the most helpful spiritual disciplines you can ever undertake. By prayerfully memorizing a verse, you will spend time with God. The verse written on your heart will help you resist temptation and inform your whole life. What better time to begin memorizing than Lent?

Suggested passages for memorization appear below, but feel free to choose any verse or passage that appeals to you or challenges you. Whatever Scripture passage you choose, make it your own by inserting "I" or "me" in place of "you" or "us." For example, "For sin will have no dominion over [me], since [I am] not under the law" (Romans 6:14).

With memorization, less is more. Pick one or two passages that really speak to you, and work on them every day. As with learning a language, it is repetition that implants the words in your head and heart. A daily time commitment is the only way to memorize anything long term. What is rapidly memorized rapidly disappears! As part of your prayer time each day, repeat your chosen verse until you have it down perfectly. Continue repeating the old one to yourself every day even after you have moved on to a new verse.

Against temptation:

- For sin will have no dominion over you, since you are not under law but under grace. (Romans 6:14)

- God is our refuge and strength, / a very present help in trouble. (Psalm 46:1)

- Wait for the LORD; / be strong, and let your heart take courage; / yea, wait for the LORD! (Psalm 27:14)

God's promises:

- For I know the plans I have for you, says the LORD, plans for welfare and not for evil, to give you a future and a hope. Then you will call upon me and come and pray to me, and I will hear you. You will seek me and find me; when you seek me with all your heart, I will be found by you, says the LORD. (Jeremiah 29:11-14)

- For the mountains may depart and the hills be removed, / but my steadfast love shall not depart from you, / and my covenant of peace shall not be removed, / says the LORD, who has compassion on you. (Isaiah 54:10)

This Week's Readings
Monday: Lv 19:1-2, 11-18 • Ps 19:8-10, 15 • Mt 25:31-46
Tuesday: Is 55:10-11 • Ps 34:4-7, 16-19 • Mt 6:7-15
Wednesday: Jon 3:1-10 • Ps 51:3-4, 12-13, 18-19 • Lk 11:29-32
Thursday: Est C:12, 14-16, 23-25 • Ps 138:1-3, 7-8 • Mt 7:7-12
Friday: Ez 18:21-28 • Ps 130:1-8 • Mt 5:20-26
Saturday: Dt 26:16-19 • Ps 119:1-2, 4-5, 7-8 • Mt 5:43-48

Ask one person to pray the following prayer aloud slowly.

In the name of the Father, and of the Son, and of the Holy Spirit.

Although God lives in the souls of men who are unconscious of Him, how can I say that I have found Him and found myself in Him if I never know Him or think of Him, never take any interest in Him or seek Him or desire His presence in my soul?

What good does it do to say a few formal prayers to Him and then turn away and give all my mind and all my will to created things, desiring only ends that fall short of Him?

Even though my soul may be justified, yet if my mind does not belong to Him, then I do not belong to Him either.

If my love does not reach out toward Him but scatters itself in His creation, it is because I have reduced His life in me to the level of a formality, forbidding it to move me with a truly vital influence. [1]

(Pause)

Leader | Please finish praying the prayer aloud.

Jesus, Lord, you were tempted as we are.

Everything we experience, you

experienced.

You know our trials and temptations,

our fears and hopes.

Please be close to us this week as we seek

to know you

and love you more.

Holy Spirit, guide our words and thoughts.

Prompt us when we need it.

Inspire us with the fire of God's love.

Comfort our fears and anxieties.

We pray these things in Jesus' name.

Amen.

[1]Reprinted from *New Seeds of Contemplation* by Thomas Merton (New York: New Directions), 1972, pp. 43–44.

2ⁿᵈ

Sunday of Lent

Listening to God

And a voice came out of the cloud, saying, "This is my Son, my Chosen; listen to him!"

—Luke 9:35

Ask one person to pray the following prayer aloud slowly.

In the name of the Father, and of the Son, and of the Holy Spirit.

Holy God, eternal wisdom,
   before all things were made,
   you were,
   and all things were made by you.
Without beginning or end your
   goodness reigns
   in heaven and on earth.
You forever watch all creation,
   forever inspire your people with
   wisdom and love.

Lift us up, we pray, O Lord,
   so that our hearts may rise to you,
   to the supreme, unseen eternal
   and infinite One.
Lift us up to the splendid height of
   your words, mysterious,
   and inspired.

Lift us up to your mysteries, hidden in
    darkness,
    darkness profound and brilliant,
    empty, like Jesus, yet full of glory,
    the place deeply quiet and wise.
You make what is ultimate and beyond
    brightness to secretly shine in our darkness.
Your unseen ways fill to the full with most
    beautiful splendor
    the souls of those who close their eyes,
    that they may see.

And I who long to love beyond my finite mind,
    ask in this prayer that you fill me to the full,
    with what I may be allowed to see
    of your unending splendorous love.[1]
    Amen.

[1]Adapted from "St. Denis's Prayer," *Pursuit of Wisdom and Other Works
by the Author of the Cloud of Unknowing, Classics of Western Spirituality*
(Mahwah, NJ: Paulist Press), 1988, pp. 74–75.

1. Have you ever felt you were in a time of darkness, waiting on God to provide direction or answers to counter your confusion? Did you receive an answer? If so, in what way?

2. What were you taught by your parents and family or in religious education about listening to God?

Ask one person to read the Scripture passage aloud.

Genesis 15:5-12, 17-18

⁵ And he brought him outside and said, "Look toward heaven, and number the stars, if you are able to number them." Then he said to him, "So shall your descendants be." ⁶ And he believed the LORD; and he reckoned it to him as righteousness.

⁷ And he said to him, "I am the LORD who brought you from Ur of the Chaldeans, to give you this land to possess." ⁸ But he said, "O Lord GOD, how am I to know that I shall possess it?" ⁹ He said to him, "Bring me a heifer three years old, a she-goat three years old, a ram three years old, a turtledove, and a young pigeon." ¹⁰ And he brought him all these, cut them in two, and laid each half over against the other; but he did not cut the birds in two. ¹¹ And when birds of prey came down upon the carcasses, Abram drove them away.

¹² As the sun was going down, a deep sleep fell on Abram; and lo, a dread and great darkness fell upon him. . . .

¹⁷ When the sun had gone down and it was dark, behold, a smoking fire pot and a flaming torch passed between these pieces. ¹⁸ On that day the LORD made a covenant with Abram, saying, "To your descendants I give this land, from the river of Egypt to the great river, the river Euphrates. "

3. What does God give credit to Abram for? Why might this be important?

4. Abram has asked God for something. What did he ask for?

5. What comes over Abram as he sleeps?

6. How does the fear Abram experiences differ from other types of fear? Why do you think he feels this way?

7. Abram's dream or vision seals a covenant between God and Abram. A covenant binds relationships. People or groups of people agree to fulfill aspects of the relationship in particular ways. Would you describe any of your relationships as a "covenant"? What do those relationships require of you? Of the other person?

8. Do you understand your relationship to God as a covenant? How might this be helpful?

Ask one person to read the Scripture passage aloud.

Luke 9:28-36

[28] Now about eight days after these sayings he took with him Peter and John and James, and went up on the mountain to pray. [29] And as he was praying, the appearance of his countenance was altered, and his raiment became dazzling white. [30] And behold, two men talked with him, Moses and Elijah, [31] who appeared in glory and spoke of his departure, which he was to accomplish at Jerusalem. [32] Now Peter and those who were with him were heavy with sleep but kept awake, and they saw his glory and the two men who stood with him. [33] And as the men were parting from him, Peter said to Jesus, "Master, it is well that we are here; let us make three booths, one for you and one for Moses and one for Elijah"—not knowing what he said. [34] As he said this, a cloud came and overshadowed them; and they were afraid as they entered the cloud. [35] And a voice came out of the cloud, saying, "This is my Son, my Chosen; listen to him!" [36] And when the voice had spoken, Jesus was found alone. And they kept silence and told no one in those days anything of what they had seen.

9. What is it like to be "heavy with sleep" (verse 32)? How does it affect your perceptions?

10. What is happening when Peter, James, and John wake up? What do you think Peter wants to accomplish with his offer to build booths or tabernacles?

11. What happens instead of booth building? What directions does God give?

12. What do you think God wants for the situation? How does that compare to what Peter wants?

13. What helps you to listen to God? What can hinder hearing God?

14. Both Abram and the apostles experience supernatural communication in the cloud or darkness. Have you ever felt that you were in a cloud and couldn't see what was happening, couldn't figure out how to act or what to do? How did that time ultimately affect your spiritual life?

15. What parallels do you see between these two readings? List the similarities. What does God ask of Abram and the three disciples? Compare Abram's and Peter's reactions to God.

16. Do their reactions seem like prayer to you? If yes, why? If no, why not? What makes a prayer truly a prayer?

We can learn to listen to God. For most of us, it doesn't come naturally, the way asking God for assistance does. In John 10:27, Jesus is very specific: "My sheep hear my voice, and I know them, and they follow me." Following Jesus means learning to listen to him, as God told the apostles when they were in the cloud. These exercises are designed to help you find a way that comes naturally to you to "listen to him" (Luke 9:35).

Most of us long for God to give us the kind of concrete promises or directions he gave to Abram and to the apostles during the transfiguration. Few of us, however, give God the kind of time and attention that make in-depth communication possible in any relationship. Our God isn't a god of superficialities. A word from the Lord rarely comes in the midst of rushing around a store or driving on a freeway, unless we already recognize his voice from regular deep conversations—prayer.

It is only possible to listen to God if we give God time. Can you listen to someone if you don't spend time with that person? Of course not! Find time for God, free of other distractions. You know what it's like to talk to someone who is texting or whose mind is obviously elsewhere. You do not feel heard. You are speaking, but the other person's attention is on something else.

Listening in prayer starts with giving God attention, which is much more difficult than giving attention to what is visible before you, be it a person or something that needs to be done, like housework or studies. Learning to listen to God involves finding a way that you can best keep your attention focused on the God you cannot see.

First, we need to build up our trust that God is always communicating with us. We rarely listen—sometimes just because we haven't learned how to listen, or at other times because we don't really believe that God wants to communicate with us. If you fit into the latter category, it may be helpful to meditate on Revelation 3:20 in preparation for listening prayer: "Behold, I stand at the door and knock; if any one hears my voice and opens the door, I will come in to him and eat with him, and he with me."

Many styles of attending to God are provided in Appendix C. Their main purpose is to help us quiet ourselves. God speaks in a "still small voice" (1 Kings 19:12). Your goal this week is to find what helps you become sufficiently still to hear that small voice. Try the method that most appeals to you in the appendix, or try them all to find which works best for you.

Different content is provided on the following pages for each day to help facilitate your conversation with God, but you may have other topics that you need to discuss with him. Feel free to modify the subject matter, but be sure to build in listening time.

**Content for Listening Conversations with God:
Seeking a Word from the Lord**

Insert the specific content for each day at some point during your prayer. Only five days are provided because you may need extra time for one of the topics.

- DAY 1: Rest in God. Simply ask God to give your soul rest during the prayer time.

- DAY 2: If some area of your life is troubled, bring that problem to God. Do not immediately ask God to fix it or give you an answer to the problem. Just hold up the trouble, concern, or fear to God. Be with God in your difficulty. If you do not have a troubled area in your life, ask God to show you which areas of your life need attention, even though you may not be aware of it.

- DAY 3: Ask the Lord to bring to your attention anything within you that prevents you from attending to or hearing God's voice. For example, do you have fears of God that you may have never even articulated to yourself? Is there some sinfulness, an area of yourself or your life, that you want God to stay out of?

  Often when we make such a request, our mind wanders, as the mind is prone to do, and then we suddenly notice we are thinking and become aware of the contents of our thoughts.

That content can be God drawing your attention to what needs attending, what stands between you and God. We may desire dramatic manifestations, but most often God works in much more subtle ways.

If something is revealed to you, do not try to solve the problem mentally. Most of our mental energy is wasted and spent uselessly on worrying or obsessing over issues. Simply be with God as you sit, walk, or write about whatever God has brought to your attention.

- DAY 4: Ask the Lord for a specific word or sense about whatever it is that prevents you from hearing God's voice (Day 3 topic). God's response to this can be very immediate. Sometimes, in the quiet, a word will pop into your head during prayer, sometimes even a whole sentence. Sometimes a familiar phrase from Scripture or the liturgy will return to you insistently. Other times, later in the day, a word written or said will arrest your attention in an unusual way. Sometimes God will send you to the Scriptures. Be open to whatever way God chooses to communicate with you, and then write it down. If you feel that nothing comes, thank God that he does not reveal to you what you are not ready to hear, and try again another time.

- DAY 5: If you received a word or phrase from God on Day 4, take that word back to prayer, and ask God to help you understand what it means for you. Ask God if there is some way this word relates to the trouble or problem about which you prayed on Day 2. If there doesn't seem to be a relationship, bring that difficulty before God again. Ask for a word that will help you know how to live with or address the problem.

This Week's Readings

Monday: Dn 9:4-10 • Ps 79:8-9, 11, 13 • Lk 6:36-38

Tuesday: Is 1:10, 16-20 • Ps 50:8-9, 16-17, 21, 23
• Mt 23:1-12

Wednesday: Jer 18:18-20 • Ps 31:5-6, 14-16 • Mt 20:17-28

Thursday: Jer 17:5-10 • Ps 1:1-4, 6 • Lk 16:19-31

Friday: Gn 37:3-4, 12-13, 17-28 • Ps 105:16-21
• Mt 21:33-43, 45-46

Saturday: Mi 7:14-15, 18-20 • Ps 103:1-4, 9-12
• Lk 15:1-3, 11-32

Ask one person to pray the following prayer aloud slowly.

In the name of the Father, and of the Son, and of the Holy Spirit.

Lord God, you have told us to listen
   to Jesus,
your beloved Son.
Jesus, we long to hear your voice,
to follow in your way;
but we are so often self-absorbed
or distracted,
or our faith is weak.
Help us to dwell deeply in your heart,
   O Christ,
so that your Holy Spirit may dwell in us.
Strengthen us to pray in new ways this
   week,
ways that will help us hear your voice,
ways that will show us your way.
Help us to shape ourselves
that you may speak within us,
that we may be yours,
and you ours.
We ask this through Christ our Lord,
Who lives and reigns forever and ever.

Amen.

3rd

Sunday of Lent
The Fruit of Freedom

For freedom Christ has set us free;
stand fast therefore, and do not submit
again to a yoke of slavery.

—Galatians 5:1

Ask one person to pray the following prayer aloud slowly.

In the name of the Father, and of the Son, and of the Holy Spirit.

Jesus, help us to call to mind your presence, for you promised to be with us when two or more are gathered in your name. Holy Spirit, we ask you to pray in us as we pray this prayer.

O Lord my God,
teach my heart this day where and how to see you,
where and how to find you.
You have made me and remade me,
and you have bestowed on me
all the good things I possess,
and still I do not know you.
I have not yet done that
for which I was made.

Teach me to seek you,
for I cannot seek you
unless you teach me,
or find you
unless you show yourself to me.
Let me seek you in my desire;
let me desire you in my seeking.
Let me find you by loving you;
let me love you when I find you.[1]
Amen.

[1]Adapted from the *Proslogion* (Discourse on the Existence of God), written in 1077–1078 by St. Anselm. The entire discourse can be found at http://www.stanselminstitute.org/files/AnselmProslogion.pdf.

1. In Catholic understanding, freedom is not merely the ability to choose between this or that action, but rather the ability to love. How is this idea of freedom different from the way most people think of freedom?

Ask one person to read the Scripture passage aloud.

Exodus 3:1-15

¹Now Moses was keeping the flock of his father-in-law, Jethro, the priest of Midian; and he led his flock to the west side of the wilderness, and came to Horeb, the mountain of God. ² And the angel of the LORD appeared to him in a flame of fire out of the midst of a bush; and he looked, and lo, the bush was burning, yet it was not consumed. ³ And Moses said, "I will turn aside and see this great sight, why the bush is not burnt." ⁴ When the LORD saw that he turned aside to see, God called to him out of the bush, "Moses, Moses!" And he said, "Here am I." ⁵ Then he said, "Do not come near; put off your shoes from your feet, for the place on which you are standing is holy ground." ⁶ And he said, "I am the God of your father, the God of Abraham, the God of Isaac, and the God of Jacob." And Moses hid his face, for he was afraid to look at God.

⁷ Then the LORD said, "I have seen the affliction of my people who are in Egypt, and have heard their cry because of their taskmasters; I know their sufferings, ⁸ and I have come down to deliver them out of the hand

of the Egyptians, and to bring them up out of that land to a good and broad land, a land flowing with milk and honey, to the place of the Canaanites, the Hittites, the Amorites, the Perizzites, the Hivites, and the Jebusites. ⁹ And now, behold, the cry of the people of Israel has come to me, and I have seen the oppression with which the Egyptians oppress them. ¹⁰ Come, I will send you to Pharaoh that you may bring forth my people, the sons of Israel, out of Egypt." ¹¹ But Moses said to God, "Who am I that I should go to Pharaoh, and bring the sons of Israel out of Egypt?" ¹² He said, "But I will be with you; and this shall be the sign for you, that I have sent you: when you have brought forth the people out of Egypt, you shall serve God upon this mountain."

¹³ Then Moses said to God, "If I come to the people of Israel and say to them, 'The God of your fathers has sent me to you,' and they ask me, 'What is his name?' what shall I say to them?" ¹⁴ God said to Moses, "I AM WHO I AM." And he said, "Say this to the people of Israel, 'I am has sent me to you.'" ¹⁵ God also said to Moses, "Say this to the people of Israel, 'The LORD, the God of your fathers, the God of Abraham, the God of Isaac, and the God of Jacob, has sent me to you': this is my name for ever, and thus I am to be remembered throughout all generations."

2. How would you summarize the situation of the Israelites at this time in their history?

3. Which words and images describe God's attitude toward the Israelites?

4. Looking at God's words and actions in this passage, how would you describe the Lord's treatment of Moses?

5. Have you ever felt inadequate for something you felt called to do? What happened? What fruit came from trusting God through the challenge or difficulty?

Ask one person to read the Scripture passage aloud.

Luke 13:1-9

[1]There were some present at that very time who told him of the Galileans whose blood Pilate had mingled with their sacrifices. [2]And he answered them, "Do you think that these Galileans were worse sinners than all the other Galileans, because they suffered thus? [3]I tell you, No; but unless you repent you will all likewise perish. [4]Or those eighteen upon whom the tower in Siloam fell and killed them, do you think that they were worse offenders than all the others who dwelt in Jerusalem? [5]I tell you, No; but unless you repent you will all likewise perish."

[6]And he told this parable: "A man had a fig tree planted in his vineyard; and he came seeking fruit on it and found none. [7]And he said to the vinedresser, 'Lo, these three years I have come seeking fruit on this fig tree, and I find none. Cut it down; why should it use up the ground?' [8]And he answered him, 'Let it alone, sir, this year also, till I dig about it and put on manure. [9]And if it bears fruit next year, well and good; but if not, you can cut it down.'"

6. What appears to be Jesus' primary concern in this passage?

7. Jesus seems to be telling this parable in order to illustrate his teaching. How do you think the parable relates to what he taught earlier in the passage?

8. How does the vinedresser propose to save the fig tree?

9. Does the God of Exodus seem more like the owner of the vineyard or the vinedresser?

10. What does this parable say about God's attitude toward us?

11. Can you name some examples of spiritual fruit? Or can you describe someone whose spiritual life and faith seem to be fruitful?

12. What in your life seems to impede your ability to draw nutrients and bear fruit?

13. What practical steps can you take to eliminate these impediments?

14. Who or what in your life nourishes you spiritually? What fruit can you see from that nourishment?

15. What connections can you make between the first reading and the Gospel?

Take a few days this week to prayerfully read through this quote from the *Catechism of the Catholic Church* about freedom and God's glory, and reflect on the questions provided.

> The glory of God consists in the realization of this manifestation and communication of his goodness, for which the world was created. God made us "to be his sons through Jesus Christ, according to the purpose of his will, *to the praise of his glorious grace*" (Ephesians 1:5-6) for "the glory of God is man fully alive; moreover man's life is the vision of God: if God's revelation through creation has already obtained life for all the beings that dwell on earth, how much more will the Word's manifestation of the Father obtain life for those who see God" (St. Irenaeus, *Adv. haeres* 4, 20, 7: PG 7/1, 1037). The ultimate purpose of creation is that God "who is the creator of all things may at last become 'all in all,' thus simultaneously assuring his own glory and our beatitude" (Vatican II, *Ad Gentes,* 2; cf. 1 Corinthians 15:28). (294)

- How can I allow God's goodness (or glory) to shine forth in my life today?

- How can my life today be a "vision of God"?

- In what ways is my whole life a living portrait of God? In other words, in what ways does my life tell people something about who God is? What other, possibly greater changes might I have to make for this to be possible?

- How might my life in any way cause people to think less of God's goodness?

- What areas in my life are crying out for God's presence and spiritual nourishment?

- Do I hope that God will become "all in all" (cf. 1 Corinthians 15:28)? How might I grow in this hope?

Last week we worked on listening to God. This week, talk with Jesus about becoming free and bearing fruit, and then listen to what he says to you. Here are some questions you might ask him.

- How have you freed me, Jesus?

- What can I do today to increase the freedom that you long for me to have?

- What person in my life nourishes my ability to bear fruit? Is there a way that I can allow that person to help me more?

- What habits are making me fruitful?

- What habits are making me barren?

This Week's Readings

Monday: 2 Kgs 5:1-15 • Ps 42:2-3; 43:3-4 • Lk 4:24-30

Tuesday: Dn 3:25, 34-43 • Ps 25:4-9 • Mt 18:21-35

Wednesday: Dt 4:1, 5-9 • Ps 147:12-13, 15-16, 19-20 • Mt 5:17-19

Thursday: Jer 7:23-28 • Ps 95:1-2, 6-9 • Lk 11:14-23

Friday: Hos 14:2-10 • Ps 81:6-11, 14, 17 • Mk 12:28-34

Saturday: Hos 6:1-6 • Ps 51:3-4, 18-21 • Lk 18:9-14

Ask one person to pray the following prayer aloud slowly.

In the name of the Father, and of the Son, and of the Holy Spirit.

> Jesus, tender vinedresser,
> nurture our lives with your life.
> Grant us tenacity to meet you in the
>   Scriptures each day.
> Guide our growth toward the fruit you
>   wish us to bear.
> Nourish us with friends who will help us
>   to bring forth fruit.
> Water us with your Spirit in prayer.
> Strengthen our branches with good
>   works.
> Thank you for this time with you
>   together.
>
> We ask this as we pray the words that
>   you taught us:
> Our Father . . .
> **Amen.**

4th

Sunday of Lent
Embracing Forgiveness

In Christ God was reconciling the world to himself, not counting their trespasses against them, and entrusting to us the message of reconciliation.

—2 Corinthians 5:19

Pray together "antiphonally" the responsorial psalm for this coming Sunday, Psalm 34. Divide into two groups. One group reads a stanza out loud; then the next group reads the next stanza.

In the name of the Father, and of the Son, and of the Holy Spirit.

1 I will bless the LORD at all times;
his praise shall continually be in my mouth.
My soul makes its boast in the LORD;
let the afflicted hear and be glad.
O magnify the LORD with me,
and let us exalt his name together!

2 I sought the LORD, and he answered me,
and delivered me from all my fears.
Look to him, and be radiant;
so your faces shall never be ashamed.
This poor man cried, and the LORD heard him,
and saved him out of all his troubles.
The angel of the LORD encamps
around those who fear him, and delivers them.
O taste and see that the LORD is good!
Happy is the man who takes refuge in him!
O fear the LORD, you his saints,
for those who fear him have no want!
The young lions suffer want and hunger;
but those who seek the LORD lack no good thing.

Come, O sons, listen to me,
I will teach you the fear of the LORD.
What man is there who desires life,
and covets many days, that he may enjoy good?
Keep your tongue from evil,
and your lips from speaking deceit.
Depart from evil, and do good;
seek peace, and pursue it.

The eyes of the LORD are toward the righteous,
and his ears toward their cry.
The face of the LORD is against evildoers,
to cut off the remembrance of them from the earth.
When the righteous cry for help, the LORD hears,
and delivers them out of all their troubles.
The LORD is near to the brokenhearted,
and saves the crushed in spirit.

Many are the afflictions of the righteous;
but the LORD delivers him out of them all.
He keeps all his bones;
not one of them is broken.
Evil shall slay the wicked;
and those who hate the righteous will be condemned.
The LORD redeems the life of his servants;
none of those who take refuge in him will be condemned.

Glory be to the Father, and to the Son, and to the Holy Spirit,
as it was in the beginning, is now, and will be forever.
Amen.

1. Recall a time when a close friend or relative wronged you in some way. Were you able to forgive that person? If so, what helped you to forgive? If not, has the failure to forgive affected your life in any way?

Ask one person to read the Scripture passage aloud.

Luke 15:1-3, 11-32

[1] Now the tax collectors and sinners were all drawing near to hear him. [2] And the Pharisees and the scribes murmured, saying, "This man receives sinners and eats with them."

[3] So he told them this parable. . . .

[11] And he said, "There was a man who had two sons; [12] and the younger of them said to his father, 'Father, give me the share of property that falls to me.' And he divided his living between them. [13] Not many days later, the younger son gathered all he had and took his journey into a far country, and there he squandered his property in loose living. [14] And when he had spent everything, a great famine arose in that country, and he began to be in want. [15] So he went and joined himself to one of the citizens of that country, who sent him into his fields to feed swine. [16] And he would gladly have fed on the pods that the swine ate; and no one gave him anything. [17] But when he came to himself he said, 'How many of my father's hired servants have

bread enough and to spare, but I perish here with hunger! [18] I will arise and go to my father, and I will say to him, "Father, I have sinned against heaven and before you; [19] I am no longer worthy to be called your son; treat me as one of your hired servants.'" [20] And he arose and came to his father. But while he was yet at a distance, his father saw him and had compassion, and ran and embraced him and kissed him. [21] And the son said to him, 'Father, I have sinned against heaven and before you; I am no longer worthy to be called your son.' [22] But the father said to his servants, 'Bring quickly the best robe, and put it on him; and put a ring on his hand, and shoes on his feet; [23] and bring the fatted calf and kill it, and let us eat and make merry; [24] for this my son was dead, and is alive again; he was lost, and is found.' And they began to make merry.

[25] "Now his elder son was in the field; and as he came and drew near to the house, he heard music and dancing. [26] And he called one of the servants and asked what this meant. [27] And he said to him, 'Your brother has come, and your father has killed the fatted calf, because he has received him safe and sound.' [28] But he was angry and refused to go in. His father came out and entreated him, [29] but he answered his father, 'Lo, these many years I have served you, and I never disobeyed your command; yet you never gave me a kid, that I might make merry with my friends. [30] But when this son of yours came, who has devoured your living with harlots, you killed for him the fatted calf!' [31] And he said to him, 'Son, you are always with me, and all that is mine is yours. [32] It was fitting to make merry and be glad, for this your brother was dead, and is alive; he was lost, and is found.'"

2. Why do you think the younger son wanted to leave home?

3. What was his life like after he left?

4. What do you think the father meant when he said, "Your brother was dead" (verse 32)? What are the implications of that statement? What does it say about the father's attitude toward his son's decisions?

5. What are some possible interpretations or conclusions the father could have come to when he saw his son approaching the house?

6. What reaction from the father do you think would have been justified? How rational does his actual reaction seem to you?

7. How do you think the prodigal son felt in the moment when his father ran to him, embraced him, and kissed him before he even had the chance to apologize?

8. Why would the father's unconditional forgiveness of the prodigal son make the older son angry? Have you ever felt similar in a family or work situation?

9. The father said to the older son, "You are always with me, and all that is mine is yours" (verse 31). Do you think this comforted the older son? Why or why not?

10. Jesus is telling this parable to illustrate the nature of God the Father. How would you feel if God the Father spoke audibly to you, saying, "You are always with me, and all that is mine is yours"? What exactly would that mean to you?

Ask one person to read the Scripture passage aloud.

2 Corinthians 5:17-21

[17] Therefore, if any one is in Christ, he is a new creation; the old has passed away, behold, the new has come. [18] All this is from God, who through Christ reconciled us to himself and gave us the ministry of reconciliation; [19] that is, God was in Christ reconciling the world to himself, not counting their trespasses against them, and entrusting to us the message of reconciliation. [20] So we are ambassadors for Christ, God making his appeal through us. We beseech you on behalf of Christ, be reconciled to God. [21] For our sake he made him to be sin who knew no sin, so that in him we might become the righteousness of God.

11. The season of Lent is one of the times during the year when the Church intentionally relates the second reading from an epistle to the Gospel and Old Testament readings. What connections can you see between this reading and the parable of the prodigal son?

12. What might being a new creation have looked like in the prodigal son's life? What would it take for his older brother to become a new creation?

13. How would you define the word "reconciliation"?[1] What do you think it means to be reconciled with someone?

14. Dr. Robert Enright, one of the foremost scholars on the topic of forgiveness, defines forgiveness as a response of goodness or love to someone who has unjustly hurt you.[2] How is forgiveness related to reconciliation? How is it different?

15. Why do you think being reconciled to God is important for spreading the "message of reconciliation" (verse 19)? How do you think we can convey that message to our families, our society, and our world?

[1]Dictionary.com defines "reconcile" this way: "to win over to friendliness; cause to become amicable"; "to compose or settle (a quarrel, dispute, etc.)"; "to bring into agreement or harmony; make compatible or consistent."

[2]Robert Enright, PhD, is a professor of educational psychology at the University of Wisconsin, Madison, who has been studying forgiveness since 1985. For more on his insights into forgiveness, see the Forgiveness Institute website: http://internationalforgiveness.com/.

Priests are the primary ministers of reconciliation, as they administer the sacraments, but laypeople are also ambassadors for this reconciliation. We are literally sent into the world to represent Christ in interactions with those who do not know the joy of being reconciled with God. (See *Catechism of the Catholic Church*, 981.) This week try one of the concrete ways listed below to spread the message of reconciliation.

Before you can be an ambassador, however, you need to know the "country" for which you are an ambassador! We must become more familiar with the land of forgiveness and reconciliation. In view of this week's Gospel reading, *now* is an excellent time to make your own Lenten confession in the Sacrament of Reconciliation. See Appendix E for a guide to confession. When you feel forgiven yourself, a recipient of the abundant love and generosity of God, you will know of what you speak. As we become "new creations" (cf. 2 Corinthians 5:17), we will grow in sincerity, humility, and love.

- Apologize to someone you have wronged, even if you feel that you were wronged by that person first. Seek to restore or improve your relationship with that person. Think about different ways to express your sincere apology. There are more ways to show a desire for reconciliation than simply saying, "I'm sorry."

- For some people, other ways to express your apology may be much more appreciated. For example, if the person is in your life, you could give them a gift, smile at them, ask them how they are doing, or do something to serve them. If the person isn't in your life, you could send a card or possibly call, if that would be appropriate. If the person has passed away, you could pray for them, visit their grave, or have a Mass said for them.

- Commit to working on forgiving one person who has wronged you. It can be a big or small offense, even something very small. Just concentrate on one offense by one person. Forgiveness does not always start with a feeling; it often starts with the decision to work on the desire to forgive. Like the father of the prodigal son, try not to put any condition on your forgiving. Oftentimes those who have wronged you will never apologize and will never change. They may even have already died. Forgiveness is an act of mercy, a response to the mercy we have received from Jesus. In Appendix D, you will find a guide with some suggestions to help you with the process of forgiveness.

This is difficult work! Unite any difficulties or sufferings you experience to Jesus Christ on the cross and ask him to help you repent, apologize, and forgive.

This Week's Readings

Monday: Is 65:17-21 • Ps 30:2, 4-6, 11-13 • Jn 4:43-54

Tuesday: Ez 47:1-9, 12 • Ps 46:2-3, 5-6, 8-9 • Jn 5:1-16

Wednesday: Is 49:8-15 • Ps 145:8-9, 13-14, 17-18 • Jn 5:17-30

Thursday: Ex 32:7-14 • Ps 106:19-23 • Jn 5:31-47

Friday: Wis 2:1, 12-22 • Ps 34:17-21, 23 • Jn 7:1-2, 10, 25-30

Saturday: Jer 11:18-20 • Ps 7:2-3, 9-12 • Jn 7:40-53

Ask one person to read the following paragraph aloud. Allow a time of silence; then slowly pray the closing prayer.

In Romans 9, St. Paul wrote about God patiently making his people into "vessels of mercy," prepared to "make known the riches of his glory" (verse 23).

Let's take a moment of silence to think about what would need to change in our hearts for each one of us to become a vessel of mercy. **(Silence)**

In the name of the Father, and of the Son, and of the Holy Spirit.

Lord, we have difficulty even wanting to be vessels of mercy when our hearts have been wounded and broken.

Showing mercy—even to those who have hurt us, betrayed us, lied to us, rejected us—requires more love than we have in our hearts.

Yet you said, "Blessed are the merciful, for they shall obtain mercy" (Matthew 5:7).

We know we need your mercy, Lord.

You showed us the greatness of the Father's love, Jesus,
   putting aside your divinity,
   coming to us in "the form of a servant,
   being born in the likeness of men"
(Philippians 2:7).

Thank you for being God's mercy for us, Jesus, despite the cost. For while we were still sinners, you died for us (cf. Romans 5:8).

Give us the desire to die to ourselves if that is what it takes to make us merciful, Jesus.

Fill us with the Father's love and mercy that gave us you, so great a savior.

Make us "vessels of mercy," people worthy to "make known the riches of your glory."

We cannot do this without you, Jesus.

We need the Holy Spirit to forgive the unforgivable, to love as you loved.

We trust you will do this, Jesus, because of your mercy.
Amen.

Close with the Glory Be.

5th

Sunday of Lent

Press On Toward the Goal

But one thing I do, forgetting what lies behind and straining forward to what lies ahead, I press on toward the goal for the prize of the upward call of God in Christ Jesus.

—Philippians 3:13-14

Ask one person to pray the following prayer aloud slowly.

In the name of the Father, and of the Son, and of the Holy Spirit.

Lord Jesus, let me know myself and know you,
And desire nothing save only you.
Let me hate myself and love you.
Let me do everything for the sake of you.
Let me humble myself and exalt you.
Let me think nothing except you.
Let me die to myself and live in you.
Let me accept whatever happens as from you.
Let me banish self and follow you,
and ever desire to follow you.
Let me fly from myself and take refuge in you,
that I may deserve to be defended by you.
Let me fear for myself, let me fear you,
and let me be among those who are chosen
   by you.
Let me distrust myself and put my trust in you.
Let me be willing to obey for the sake of you.
Let me cling to nothing save only to you,
and let me be poor because of you.
Look upon me, that I may love you.
Call me that I may see you,
And forever enjoy you.
Amen.

—A prayer attributed to St. Augustine

1. What do you think this language in the opening prayer means: "Let me hate myself"? What do you think of it?

2. Have you ever gained something at great personal cost, something that required real sacrifice? Would you say it was worth it?

Ask one person to read the Scripture passage aloud.

Philippians 3:8-14

[8] Indeed I count everything as loss because of the surpassing worth of knowing Christ Jesus my Lord. For his sake I have suffered the loss of all things, and count them as refuse, in order that I may gain Christ [9] and be found in him, not having a righteousness of my own, based on law, but that which is through faith in Christ, the righteousness from God that depends on faith; [10] that I may know him and the power of his resurrection, and may share his sufferings, becoming like him in his death, [11] that if possible I may attain the resurrection from the dead.

[12] Not that I have already obtained this or am already perfect; but I press on to make it my own, because Christ Jesus has made me his own. [13] Brethren, I do not consider that I have made it my own; but one thing I do, forgetting what lies behind and straining forward to what lies ahead, [14] I press on

toward the goal for the prize of the upward call of God in Christ Jesus.

3. How would you describe the overall tone of this passage? What emotions does it convey to you?

4. In various ways, Paul refers to the hopes he has regarding his relationship with Christ (for example, in verse 8 he says, "in order that I may gain Christ"). What are some of the other hopes he expresses? Do you personally resonate with any of these?

5. St. Paul writes that he wants to share in Christ's sufferings. Can you see any hints in the passage that indicate what he has in mind?

6. What does it mean to you to share in the sufferings of Christ (verse 10)?

7. Thinking about anything you know that "lies behind" in St. Paul's life, what do you think Paul means by "forgetting what lies behind" (verse 13)?

8. Are there any sins that, through great struggle and the grace of God, you have left behind? If you feel comfortable, please share this work of grace with the group.

9. What are you feeling called to leave behind? Is there anything that keeps you from pressing forward to the prize?

Ask one person to read the Scripture passage aloud.

John 8:1-11

[1]Jesus went to the Mount of Olives. [2]Early in the morning he came again to the temple; all the people came to him, and he sat down and taught them. [3]The scribes and the Pharisees brought a woman who had been caught in adultery, and placing her in the midst [4]they said to him, "Teacher, this woman has been caught in the act of adultery. [5]Now in the law Moses commanded us to stone such. What do you say about her?" [6]This they said to test him, that they might have some charge to bring against him. Jesus bent down and wrote with his finger on the ground. [7]And as they continued to ask him, he stood up and said to them, "Let him who is without sin among you be the first to throw a stone at her." [8]And once more he bent down and wrote with his finger on the ground. [9]But when they heard it, they went away, one by one, beginning with the eldest, and Jesus was left alone with the woman standing before him. [10]Jesus looked up and said to her, "Woman, where are they? Has no one condemned you?" [11]She said, "No one, Lord." And Jesus said, "Neither do I condemn you; go, and do not sin again."

10. How does the Gospel reading connect to the reading from Philippians?

11. Clearly, the Pharisees took the woman's sin seriously. What was wrong with their reaction to the woman?

12. Do you think Jesus took this woman's sin seriously? Why or why not?

13. How do we take our sin seriously and at the same time accept God's forgiveness?

14. Have you ever struggled to accept God's forgiveness or to forgive yourself? If so, and if you feel comfortable sharing about it, how were you able to work through it and receive the mercy Jesus offers?

15. How do we call sin "sin" and yet not condemn a person? Has anyone ever talked to you about your sin in such a way that you didn't feel condemned? How did that affect you?

16. How do you think the woman felt when Jesus uttered his last words to her (verse 11)? How do you see the rest of the woman's life unfolding? How have you felt after receiving God's mercy?

In order to continue pressing on, it will be helpful to spend another week planting God's word in our minds and hearts. Read each of these short passages on perseverance:

- 1 Corinthians 9:24-27 (run the race)
- Ephesians 6:10-18 (sometimes all we are supposed to do is stand)
- 1 Peter 5:8-11 (God is just around the corner)
- James 1:2-4 (be joyful and steadfast in trials)
- 1 Corinthians 10:13 (God helps us in temptation)
- James 1:12 (those who endure will win the crown)
- 1 Corinthians 16:13 (be courageous and strong)

Choose one verse to memorize so that God can use his word to help you press on when you're discouraged. (If you need to be convinced this is worth the trouble, go back to Week 1 of this study, the First Sunday of Lent.) Also, notice how Jesus uses God's word when he is tempted by Satan in the desert (Luke 4:1-13). See also Psalm 119:9-11, where the psalmist speaks about how he fortifies himself with God's word.

- Counting everything else as loss compared to knowing Christ (cf. Philippians 3:8) happens only when we have truly entered into an authentic, loving, and joyful relationship with Jesus.

Spend some time with the passages on the previous page, looking for reasons to love God (engaging your mind) and then expressing your love for God (engaging your heart).

* For a great example of perseverance and giving up all for Christ, read *The Hiding Place*, Corrie ten Boom's account of her family's resistance to the Nazis during World War II and their subsequent imprisonment for hiding Jews. She speaks of discovering God's riches even in the darkest places.

This Week's Readings

Monday: Dn 13:1-9, 15-17, 19-30, 33-62 • Ps 23:1-6 • Jn 8:1-11
Tuesday: Nm 21:4-9 • Ps 102:2-3, 16-21 • Jn 8:21-30
Wednesday: Dn 3:14-20, 91-92, 95 • (Ps) Dn 3:52-56 • Jn 8:31-42
Thursday: Gn 17:3-9 • Ps 105:4-9 • Jn 8:51-59
Friday: Jer 20:10-13 • Ps 18:2-7 • Jn 10:31-42
Saturday: Ez 37:21-28 • (Ps) Jer 31:10-13 • Jn 11:45-56

Pray the following prayer aloud together.

In the name of the Father, and of the Son, and of the Holy Spirit.

Lord, teach me to be generous.
Teach me to serve you as you deserve;
to give and not to count the cost,
to fight and not to heed the wounds,
to toil and not to seek for rest,
to labor and not to ask for reward,
save that of knowing that I do your
will. **Amen.**

—A prayer attributed to St. Ignatius of Loyola

Palm Sunday
of the Lord's Passion
Jesus, Remember Me

"Satan demanded to have
you, that he might sift
you like wheat."
　　　　　—Luke 22:31

Below is the second reading from Sunday's liturgy of the passion. This passage from Philippians may have been an early Christian hymn.

Ask one person to pray the Scripture aloud slowly, and another to pray the prayer below it.

In the name of the Father, and of the Son, and of the Holy Spirit.

Have this mind among yourselves,
which was in Christ Jesus,
who, though he was in the form of God,
did not count equality with God a thing to be grasped,
but emptied himself, taking the form of a servant,
being born in the likeness of men.
And being found in human form
he humbled himself and became obedient unto death,
even death on a cross.
Therefore God has highly exalted him and bestowed on him the name which is above every name,

that at the name of Jesus every knee should bow,
in heaven and on earth and under the earth,
and every tongue confess that Jesus Christ is Lord, to the
glory of God the Father. (Philippians 2:5-11)

Holy Spirit, you lead us to confess Jesus Christ as Lord.
Guide and inspire our hearts and minds as we gather to reflect
on our Lord's passion.
Open our hearts so that we may hear you speak to us
through your holy word.
Father, please intensify our love for your Son
by increasing our desire to do his will in our lives.
We pray this through Christ our Lord.
Amen.

1. Is there a person in your life, the story of a particular saint, or even a scene from a book or movie that has inspired you to want to sacrifice yourself for God and others? Would someone be willing to share about this?

The full Gospel reading for Passion Sunday is Luke 22:14–23:56. The discussion questions address only the text that appears below. You may wish to open a Bible to the full passage in case you have questions on verses not included here.

Ask one person to read the Scripture passage aloud.

$^{22:14}$ And when the hour came, he sat at table, and the apostles with him. ^{15} And he said to them, "I have earnestly desired to eat this Passover with you before I suffer; ^{16} for I tell you I shall not eat it until it is fulfilled in the kingdom of God." ^{17} And he took a cup, and when he had given thanks he said, "Take this, and divide it among yourselves; ^{18} for I tell you that from now on I shall not drink of the fruit of the vine until the kingdom of God comes." ^{19} And he took bread, and when he had given thanks he broke it and gave it to them, saying, "This is my body which is given for you. Do this in remembrance of me." ^{20} And likewise the cup after supper, saying, "This cup which is poured out for you is the new covenant in my blood."

2. Here is the Last Supper and the institution of the Eucharist. Reread verses 15-16, which are unique to Luke. What is Jesus conveying here? How do you think Jesus felt as he shared this last meal with his disciples?

3. What might the disciples have thought as Jesus, blessing the bread and wine, seemed to foretell what would happen to him (verse 18)? Do you think they understood the implications of what he was saying? Have you ever had a time when someone said something extremely significant that you only later recognized was full of meaning?

Ask one person to read the Scripture passage aloud.

22:24 A dispute also arose among them, which of them was to be regarded as the greatest. 25 And he said to them, "The kings of the Gentiles exercise lordship over them; and those in authority over them are called benefactors. 26 But not so with you; rather let the greatest among you become as the youngest, and the leader as one who serves. 27 For which is the greater, one who sits at table, or one who serves? Is it not the one who sits at table? But I am among you as one who serves.

28 "You are those who have continued with me in my trials; 29 as my Father appointed a kingdom for me, so do I appoint for you 30 that you may eat and drink at my table in my kingdom, and sit on thrones judging the twelve tribes of Israel."

4. This dispute among the apostles during the Last Supper is also unique to Luke. Why do you think he might have included this dispute about greatness?

5. What does it say about the state of the apostles' minds that they were arguing in this way?

6. How do you think the apostles felt about this conversation later, after the crucifixion?

7. When are you most tempted to be worried about your status?

8. If even the apostles were focused on their personal glory during the Last Supper, what does that indicate about us?

Ask one person to read the Scripture passage aloud.

22:31"Simon, Simon, behold, Satan demanded to have you, that he might sift you like wheat, 32 but I have prayed for you that your faith may not fail; and when you have turned again, strengthen your brethren." 33 And he said to him, "Lord, I am ready to go with you to prison and to death." 34 He said, "I tell you, Peter, the cock will not crow this day, until you three times deny that you know me."

9. Sifting wheat isn't like sifting flour, which requires only gentle shaking or stirring. Threshing wheat (as we would call it) requires violent beating to separate the grain (wheat berry) from the stalk and the chaff. The wheat is literally

torn apart. How does this affect your understanding of what Jesus says to Peter (verse 31)?

10. What does Jesus' warning to Peter tell us about how God relates to us in our struggle with weakness and sin?

Ask one person to read the Scripture passage aloud.

22:39 And he came out, and went, as was his custom, to the Mount of Olives; and the disciples followed him. 40 And when he came to the place he said to them, "Pray that you may not enter into temptation." 41 And he withdrew from them about a stone's throw, and knelt down and prayed, 42 "Father, if thou art willing, remove this cup from me; nevertheless not my will, but thine, be done." 43 And there appeared to him an angel from heaven, strengthening him. 44 And being in an agony he prayed more earnestly; and his sweat became like great drops of blood falling down upon the ground. 45 And when he rose from prayer, he came to the disciples and found them sleeping for sorrow, 46 and he said to them, "Why do you sleep? Rise and pray that you may not enter into temptation."

11. What do you think Jesus feared as he agonized in the garden?

12. The description "sweat . . . like great drops of blood falling down upon the ground" (verse 44) is unique to Luke. What does this add to your understanding of the agony in the garden?

13. Jesus advises the disciples to pray so that they won't "enter into temptation" (verse 46). What kind of temptations do you think would assail the apostles at this time?

Ask one person to read the Scripture passage aloud.

[47] While he was still speaking, there came a crowd, and the man called Judas, one of the twelve, was leading them. He drew near to Jesus to kiss him; [48] but Jesus said to him, "Judas, would you betray the Son of man with a kiss?" [49] And when those who were about him saw what would follow, they said, "Lord, shall we strike with the sword?" [50] And one of them struck the slave of the high priest and cut off his right ear. [51] But Jesus said, "No more of this!" And he touched his ear and healed him. [52] Then Jesus said to the chief priests and captains of the temple and elders, who had come out against him, "Have you come out as against a robber, with swords and clubs? [53] When I was with you day after day in the temple, you did not lay hands on me. But this is your hour, and the power of darkness."

[54] Then they seized him and led him away, bringing him into the high priest's house. Peter followed at a distance.

Facilitator: Read the following aloud:

Sit quietly for a moment with your eyes closed. Imagine you are Judas, approaching Jesus amid a crowd carrying torches and clubs through the night. You see Jesus ahead with his apostles. You have spent the last few years with these people.

You had hoped he was the Messiah, the one who would set Israel free from the Romans.

After a few moments of silence, ask the following questions.

14. What do you, Judas, feel when you see Jesus and the apostles?

15. How do you, Judas, feel when Jesus says, "Judas, would you betray the Son of man with a kiss" (verse 48)?

Ask one person to read the Scripture passage aloud.

23:13 Pilate then called together the chief priests and the rulers and the people, 14 and said to them, "You brought me this man as one who was perverting the people; and after examining him before you, behold, I did not find this man guilty of any of your charges against him; 15 neither did Herod, for he sent him back to us. Behold, nothing deserving death has been done by him; 16 I will therefore chastise him and release him."

18 But they all cried out together, "Away with this man, and release to us Barabbas"— 19 a man who had been thrown into prison for an insurrection started in the city, and for murder. 20 Pilate addressed them once more, desiring to release Jesus; 21 but they shouted out, "Crucify, crucify him!" 22 A third time he said to them, "Why, what evil has he done? I have found in him no crime deserving death; I will therefore chastise him and release him." 23 But they were urgent, demanding with loud cries that he should

be crucified. And their voices prevailed. [24] So Pilate gave sentence that their demand should be granted. [25] He released the man who had been thrown into prison for insurrection and murder, whom they asked for; but Jesus he delivered up to their will.

16. What motivated Pilate to give in to the demands of the crowd?

17. Have you ever given in to the demands of a group and did something you didn't want to do? How did you feel afterward? How do you think Pilate might have felt?

Ask one person to read the Scripture passage aloud.

[24:39] One of the criminals who were hanged railed at him, saying, "Are you not the Christ? Save yourself and us!" [40] But the other rebuked him, saying, "Do you not fear God, since you are under the same sentence of condemnation? [41] And we indeed justly; for we are receiving the due reward of our deeds; but this man has done nothing wrong." [42] And he said, "Jesus, remember me when you come in your kingly power." [43] And he said to him, "Truly, I say to you, today you will be with me in Paradise."

18. Look at the response of each thief to Jesus. How would you describe each of their responses? What do you think motivated them?

19. What do you think the thieves demonstrate about our salvation?

Ask one person to read the Scripture passage aloud.

When you reach the moment at verse 46 when Jesus dies, please allow a moment of silence.

24:44 It was now about the sixth hour, and there was darkness over the whole land until the ninth hour, 45 while the sun's light failed; and the curtain of the temple was torn in two. 46 Then Jesus, crying with a loud voice, said, "Father, into thy hands I commit my spirit!" And having said this he breathed his last. **(Silence)** 47 Now when the centurion saw what had taken place, he praised God, and said, "Certainly this man was innocent!" 48 And all the multitudes who assembled to see the sight, when they saw what had taken place, returned home beating their breasts. 49 And all his acquaintances and the women who had followed him from Galilee stood at a distance and saw these things.

Facilitator: Read the following meditation from St. Augustine slowly and solemnly:

As they were looking on, so we too gaze on his wounds as he hangs. We see his blood as he dies. We see the price offered by the Redeemer, touch the scars of his resurrection. He bows his head, as if to kiss you. His heart is made bare open, as it were, in love to you. His arms are extended that he may embrace you. His whole body is displayed for your redemption. Ponder how great these things are. Let all this be rightly weighed in your mind: as he was once fixed to the cross in every part of his body for you, so he may now be fixed in every part of your soul.[1]

20. What aspect of Christ's passion stands out to you most
   now that we have looked at it again?

[1]*Ancient Christian Commentary on Scripture: New Testament II.* Eds. Thomas
C. Oden and Christopher A Hall (Downers Grove, IL: InterVarsity Press),
199, p. 224.

This is Holy Week, the culmination of Lent, the high holy days of our Church. Because we prepared ourselves during the past forty days in the desert, we may now experience fully what this week means for each of us, and for the world.

These are days of "great terror, with signs and wonders" (Week 1; Deuteronomy 26:8): a meal like no other meal; men awakened in a peaceful garden to a violent mob moving toward them in the darkness with torches and clubs; the men opening their eyes to see their companion betraying their teacher with a kiss.

The "dread and great darkness" of blood and sacrifice begins (Week 2, Genesis 15:12). Caiaphas manipulates; Pilate prevaricates; Herod humiliates. All the deadly power of Rome falls onto one humble teacher who calls himself servant (Luke 22:27).

God ran to us in Christ, became human so that he could embrace us to himself as the father did the prodigal son (Week 4, Luke 15:20). He ran to us because God could not bear that we should suffer eternally in our alienation from him.

God came for us in Christ, and we killed him.

This is the Passover of the Lord. Let it set you free from bondage.

God did all this so that we might become "new creations" (Week 4; cf. 2 Corinthians 5:17); that we might not remain prisoners of sin. The Father couldn't bear that we were living wasted lives in lands far-off from him, resenting those we were given to love, accusing the brethren rather than facing our own sins (Week 4, Luke 15; Week 5, John 8). God wants so much more for his precious creation: that we become his children, working to bear fruit in the fields of the Lord (Week 3; Luke 13).

This week, enter passionately into the passion of our Lord. He has "come down to deliver" us (Week 3; Exodus 3:8). Let his passion deliver you by making you new.

Who does not want to become new? Who does not want to shed all that distorts life? Who does not want to be freed from hard, personal bondage (Week 1; Deuteronomy 26:6)? The Lord sees our enslavement (Week 3; Exodus 3:7), and he comes to set us free.

Use all the spiritual tools you have practiced this Lent to connect to the cross and Christ's passion this week. On Monday and Tuesday, fight the temptation to avoid and hide in whatever ways you naturally do.

Pray for the power of perseverance with the Scriptures that you memorized in Weeks 1 and 5. If the Scriptures you chose those weeks aren't appropriate, pick others from those sessions and memorize them.

On Wednesday, return to the exercises in Week 4. If you were facing death, whom would you need to forgive: someone who has wronged you, yourself, or someone no longer in your life or in the world?

On Holy Thursday, use the exercises that helped you listen to God in Week 2 to talk to Jesus at the Last Supper. We read John's version of the Last Supper at Mass on Holy Thursday, which includes Jesus washing the apostles' feet. Imagine Jesus washing your feet. Do you want to ask him anything? Tell him something? Speak to Jesus whatever comes into your heart.

If you are unable to attend the Holy Thursday Mass, reread Luke's description of the Last Supper (22:14-34). Give quiet time to considering that meal. Be present with Jesus there. Talk to him about what is happening and what it means for you.

On Good Friday, slowly and prayerfully reread Luke 23. This takes you from Gethsemane to Calvary. St. Ignatius taught that God can use our imaginations to plant ideas or images he wants us to consider. Imagine yourself in each scene with Jesus or with his followers.

Let your mind go to where the Holy Spirit draws you: with Jesus as he agonizes in the garden, or with the sleepy apostles who could not stay awake while their teacher and friend cried in terror. Attend the trials before Caiaphas, Pilate, and Herod. Carry your own cross up to Calvary with the Lord, or be an onlooker in the crowd.

Don't belabor the decision of who to be. Trust the Holy Spirit to guide you where you need to go.

Most important, bring your own sufferings to each scene. Like Paul, desire to share in the sufferings of Christ by finding connection points between what you suffer and what Jesus suffers (Week 5; Philippians 3:10). If this is a struggle, talk to Christ about how to do it. Ask him how to see your own suffering in his. Above all, in contemplating the crucifixion and all that leads up to it, "Listen to him" (Week 2; Luke 9:35).

If at all possible, attend the Good Friday service, which commemorates the death of the Lord on the cross—the cross that saves you.

Pray the following prayer each night before you go to sleep.

What Happened on the Cross

By nothing else except the cross of our Lord Jesus Christ
has death been brought low:
The sin of our first parent destroyed,
hell plundered,
resurrection bestowed,
the power given us to despise the things of this world,
even death itself,
the road back to the former blessedness made smooth,
the gates of paradise opened,
our nature seated at the right hand of God,
and we made children and heirs of God.
By the cross all these things have been set aright . . .
It is a seal that the destroyer may not strike us,
a raising up of those who lie fallen,
a support for those who stand,
a staff for the infirm,
a crook for the shepherded,
a guide for the wandering,
a perfecting of the advanced,
salvation for soul and body,
a deflector of all evils,
a cause of all goods,
a destruction of sin,
a plant of resurrection,
and a tree of eternal life.

—John Damascene (c. 675–749), *The Fountain of Knowledge*

This Week's Readings

Monday of Holy Week: Is 42:1-7 • Ps 27:1-3, 13-14 • Jn 12:1-11

Tuesday of Holy Week: Is 49:1-6 • Ps 71:1-6b, 15, 17 • Jn 13:21-33, 36-38

Wednesday of Holy Week: Is 50:4-9 • Ps 69:8-10, 21-22, 31, 33-34 • Mt 26:14-25

Holy Thursday: Ex 12:1-8, 11-14 • Ps 116:12-13, 15-18 • 1 Cor 11:23-26 • Jn 13:1-15

Good Friday: Is 52:13–53:12 • Ps 31:2, 6, 12-13, 15-17, 25 • Heb 4:14-16; 5:7-9 • Jn 18:1–19:42

Ask one person to read the first paragraph from Blessed Teresa of Calcutta. Ask another person to read the second paragraph, a prayer that was found in her private notebook.

After the readings, take a moment to be silent together. You may wish to allow time for spontaneous prayers of praise, thanksgiving, or petition before closing your time together.

> Suffering, pain—failure—is but a kiss of Jesus, a sign that you have come so close to Jesus on the Cross that He can kiss you. So my child be happy . . . Do not be discouraged . . . so smile back . . . For you it is a most beautiful chance of becoming fully and totally all for Jesus.[1]

> O Jesus, only love of my heart, I wish to suffer what I suffer and all Thou wilt have me suffer, for Thy pure love not because of the merits I may acquire, nor for the rewards Thou hast promised me but only to please Thee, to praise Thee, to bless Thee as well in sorrow as in joy.[2]

---

[1] Mother Teresa to a Missionary of Charity Sister, April 8, 1977. Taken from *Come Be My Light: The Private Writings of the Saint of Calcutta* (New York: Doubleday), 2007, p. 282.

[2] Prayer dictated by Jesus to Visitation Sister Benigna Consolata Ferrero (1885–1916), copied by Mother Teresa on the first page of her medical notebook in Patna, dated 1948. Taken from *Come Be My Light: The Private Writings of the Saint of Calcutta* (New York: Doubleday), 2007, p. 124.

Easter Sunday:
The Resurrection
of the Lord
**Encounter the
Risen Lord**

And they remembered his words.

—Luke 24:8

Pray the following prayer aloud together, an
Easter Prayer of Praise

**In the name of the Father, the Son, and the
Holy Spirit.**

Blessed be the God and Father
of our Lord Jesus Christ.
In his great mercy
he has given us a new birth
to a living hope through the resurrection
of Jesus Christ from the dead
and to an inheritance
that is imperishable, undefiled, and unfading.
It is reserved in heaven for you,
who because of your faith in God
are being protected by His power
until the salvation
that is ready to be revealed at the end of time.
Amen.

—Adapted from 1 Peter 1:3-5

Easter is such a great feast that it can't be celebrated on only one day. That's why the Church rejoices for eight days during the Octave of Easter that we're in now. This last meeting gives us a chance within the Easter feast to celebrate the resurrection of our Lord together and think about how the last forty days and Holy Week can shape our whole lives.

1. Which week of this Lenten study had the most impact on you? Why?

Ask one person to read the Scripture passage aloud.

1 Corinthians 5:6b-8

[6]Do you not know that a little yeast leavens the whole batch of dough? [7] Clean out the old yeast so that you may be a new batch, as you really are unleavened. For our paschal lamb, Christ, has been sacrificed. [8] Therefore, let us celebrate the festival, not with the old yeast, the yeast of malice and evil, but with the unleavened bread of sincerity and truth. (New Revised Standard Version)

2. One theme present in this reading and throughout Paul's writings is his idea of the old life before Christ and the new life in Christ. What do you see as the differences between the two?

3. How has the Lenten season allowed you to enter more fully into new life with Christ? Has it affected your relationships with others?

4. What "old yeast" have you been challenged to put away (verse 7)?

5. During this Lenten season, what tools have you found particularly helpful for growing into the new life?

Facilitator: Read the following meditation exercise aloud in a prayerful, reflective manner.

As a group, take a moment to recollect yourselves in silence and prepare your mind and heart for prayer.

To help us prepare to receive the Gospel, imagine yourself in the sandals of one of the disciples who diligently followed Jesus. **(Pause)** You gave your life to his ministry and sacrificed all that you had: your friends, your family, your livelihood, your standing as a good, observant Jew— everything! **(Pause)** Christ called you by name and gave you hope in something greater than yourself. You ardently believed that Jesus was the Messiah, the Chosen One, the Son of God. **(Pause)**

Then he died, a criminal hung upon a cross. **(Pause)**

He was ridiculed, shamed, tortured, and crucified. Think about that for a moment. **(Pause)** What feelings might you have? Betrayal? Fear? Anger? Despair?

You witnessed the miracles of a man you hoped was the Son of God. You yearned to believe in what he said. You wanted to believe he was coming back. Yet people died every day in far less brutal ways, and they did not come back.

Still, something was different about this man.

Take a few moments for reflection.

Ask one person to read the Scripture passage aloud.

Luke 24:1-12

[1]But on the first day of the week, at early dawn, they went to the tomb, taking the spices which they had prepared. [2]And they found the stone rolled away from the tomb, [3]but when they went in they did not find the body. [4]While they were perplexed about this, behold, two men stood by them in dazzling apparel; [5]and as they were frightened and bowed their faces to the ground, the men said to them, "Why do you seek the living among the dead? He is not here, but has risen. [6]Remember how he told you, while he was still in Galilee, [7]that the Son of man must be delivered into the hands of sinful men, and be crucified, and on the third day rise." [8]And they remembered his words, [9]and returning from the tomb they told all this to the eleven and to all the rest. [10]Now it was Mary Magdalene and Joanna and Mary the mother of James and the other women with them who told this to the apostles; [11]but these words seemed to them an idle tale, and they did not believe them. [12]But Peter rose and ran to the tomb; stooping and

looking in, he saw the linen cloths by themselves; and he went home wondering at what had happened.

6. What were some of the emotions that you remember experiencing in our meditation on the passion before Holy Week? What initial feelings might you experience just as you see that the stone has been rolled away?

7. What was the women's reaction to the two men who were angels? What do you think your reaction might be?

8. Can you recall a time in your life when you "remembered his words" (verse 8)? How did it change your feelings and actions?

9. Have you ever been ridiculed for sharing an experience of God? How did this affect you?

10. Did ridicule affect your trust in your own experiences of God, or your faith in God?

11. Why do you think Peter's reaction was so different from the others?

12. Peter went home amazed. When have you been amazed by Jesus' resurrected life at work in your life or in the lives of others?

We began Lent with encouragement to invite God into our lives so that we could be transformed. How do you know someone has changed? It's simple—they behave differently! Spiritual change happens interiorly but always manifests itself in our behavior.

If you have allowed God to make you a new creation, an unleavened bread of sincerity and truth, people will see the difference. You will see the difference.

While these changes in your life are real and can be long lasting, they can be lost. That is why throughout his first letter to the Corinthians, Paul exhorts the young Christians to live in Christ, that they might themselves be "the unleavened bread" (verse 8). Only living in Christ makes it possible to get rid of the "old yeast" (verse 7) day by day.

In his encyclical *Deus Caritas Est*, Pope Benedict XVI said that being a follower of Christ "is not the result of an ethical choice or a lofty idea, but the encounter with an event, a person, which gives life a new horizon and a decisive direction" (1). This is another way of saying that it is through our connection to Christ that we are made new creations each day. That connection gives our lives the "decisive direction" of one who knows and loves Jesus.

One characteristic of a life renewed and trans-formed in love is a desire for a more profound connection with others and the world. We see this all the time: lovers become spouses whose love begets children; recovering alcoholics become sponsors for the newly sober; the person who has profoundly encountered nature devotes himself to preserving God's creation.

Of this you can be sure: every one of those people must continually connect to the source of their love to keep living out that love. Spouses need time alone on dates away from the kids. Recovering alcoholics serving as sponsors receive support and renewal from their own supportive family and friends. The environmentalist returns to the quiet mountainside that she loves.

Your experiences this Lent with the methods for encountering Christ provided in "Connection to the Cross This Week" can help you, too, to return to the source of all love and beauty: God, known in Jesus Christ, the One who came to deliver us. Take the practices that have touched your life into the Easter season and the whole year. They will keep your connection to Christ strong, your horizon in sight, and your direction decisive.

Allow these practices to guide you now into greater awareness of the meaning of the resurrection. They will allow God to make you new again and again, lift you from shame and sorrow, and raise you up with him in glory. He is risen! Alleluia! Truly, resurrection is not just a concept but a lived reality for every one of us every day of our lives.

Jesus is risen, alive, and with you always, and he wants you to open yourself to encounters with him again and again, just as you did during the last forty days. He wants your relationship to grow, blossom, and bear great fruit.

Live this new life, and you will be different. You will bear that good fruit. You will see that new horizon and head for it decisively. And that newness will take you straight into a broken world full of people in desperate need of Christ's transforming love.

Living the Joy of the Resurrection throughout the Year

Here are some ways you can continue to grow in your life in Christ this year:

- Pope St. John Paul II said, "Those who have come into genuine contact with Christ cannot keep him for themselves; they must proclaim him" (*Novo Millennio Ineunte*, 40). You've connected with Jesus. Tell people! They might respond like St. Peter and go to see for themselves. They might run a long way on the journey, but ultimately, if they meet the risen Christ, they, too, will stand amazed before defeated death, full of new hope for themselves and the world.

- Review the "Connection to the Cross This Week" sections of this book to remind yourself of the words Jesus spoke to your heart this Lenten season. Pick one or two of the spiritual exercises that were most powerful for you, and commit to making them a regular part of your prayer life this coming year.

- In order to continuously "clean out the old yeast" (1 Corinthians 5:7), go to the Sacrament of Reconciliation more frequently this year. In your times of self-examination, ask the Lord to reveal any hidden "old yeast" in your life. Ask to become new unleavened dough through the grace available in the unleavened Eucharist.

- Return to the tomb often this year. Give time to sitting in the empty darkness as though it were the dark tomb that Jesus left behind. Let the full import and wonder of the Christian story amaze and captivate you. Christ has died, Christ is risen, Christ will come again!

This Week's Readings

Monday: Acts 2:14, 22-33 • Ps 16:1-2, 5, 7-11 • Mt 28:8-15
Tuesday: Acts 2:36-41 • Ps 33:4-5, 18-20, 22 • Jn 20:11-18
Wednesday: Acts 3:1-10 • Ps 105:1-4, 6-9 • Lk 24:13-35
Thursday: Acts 3:11-26 • Ps 8:2, 5-9 • Lk 24:35-48
Friday: Acts 4:1-12 • Ps 118:1-2, 4, 22-27 • Jn 21:1-14
Saturday: Acts 4:13-21 • Ps 118:1, 14-21 • Mk 16:9-15

All | Lord Jesus, you are risen from the grave.
Death has been defeated!
Alleluia, alleluia!

Reader | The women ran from the empty tomb to tell the apostles and disciples what they had seen and heard: "The tomb is empty! Jesus had said this would happen! Remember? Well, it has! He isn't dead!"

All | Lord Jesus, you are risen from the grave.
Death has been defeated!
Alleluia, alleluia!

Reader | The women couldn't go about their daily chores and tasks as though nothing had happened. Help us to be like them, driven by the glory of your resurrection in everything we do.

All | Lord Jesus, you are risen
from the grave.
Death has been defeated!
Alleluia, alleluia!

Reader | We want to live and proclaim the
truth: *Jesus is alive*! Help us tell
people about him. Help us know
we don't need fancy words or
complicated theology, just the same
kind of wonder and excitement of
the women who ran from the tomb.

All | Lord Jesus, you are risen
from the grave.
Death has been defeated!
Alleluia, alleluia!

Reader | Help us not be afraid to use your
own words to share the good news
of Jesus alive in our hearts.

All | Lord Jesus, you are risen
from the grave.
Death has been defeated!
Alleluia, alleluia!

Appendices for Participants

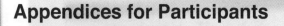

(A) Small Group Discussion Guide

(B) A Guide to Reading Scripture, Spiritual Teachers, and the Saints

(C) Learning to Listen to God

(D) The Forgiveness Process

(E) A Guide to the Sacrament of Reconciliation

Appendix  A

A small group seeks to foster an honest exploration of Jesus Christ with one another. For many, this will be a new experience. You may be wondering what will take place. Will I fit in? Will I even want to come back?

Here are some expectations and values to help participants understand how small groups work as well as what makes them work and what doesn't. When a group meets for the first time, the facilitator may want to read the following aloud and discuss it to be sure people understand small group parameters.

Purpose

We gather as searchers. Our express purpose for being here is to explore together what it means to live the gospel of Jesus Christ in and through the Church.

Priority

In order to reap the full fruit of this personal and communal journey, each one of us will make participation in the weekly gatherings a priority.

Participation

We will strive to create an environment in which all are encouraged to share at their comfort level.

Discussion Guidelines

The purpose of our gathering time is to share in "Spirit-filled" discussion. This type of dialogue occurs when the presence of the Holy Spirit is welcomed and encouraged by the nature and tenor of the discussion. To help this happen, we will observe the following guidelines:

- Participants strive always to be respectful, humble, open, and honest in listening and sharing: they don't interrupt, respond abruptly, condemn what another says, or even judge in their hearts.

- Participants share at the level that is comfortable for them personally.

- Silence is a vital part of the experience. Participants are given time to reflect before discussion begins. Keep in mind that a period of comfortable silence often occurs between individuals speaking.

- Participants are enthusiastically encouraged to share while at the same time exercising care to permit others (especially the quieter members) an opportunity to speak. Each participant should aim to maintain a balance: participating without dominating the conversation.

- Participants keep confidential anything personal that may be shared in the group.

- Perhaps most important, participants should cultivate attentiveness to the Holy Spirit's desire to be present in the time spent together. When the conversation seems to need help, ask for the Holy Spirit's intercession silently in your heart. When someone is speaking of something painful or difficult, pray that the Holy Spirit comforts that person. Pray for the Spirit to aid the group in responding sensitively and lovingly. If someone isn't participating, praying for that person during silence may be more helpful than a direct question. These are but a few examples of the ways in which each person might personally invoke the Holy Spirit.

Time

It is important that your group start and end on time. Generally a group meets for about ninety minutes, with an additional thirty minutes or so afterwards for refreshments. Agree on these times as a group, and work to honor them.

Appendix (B)

Once God gets our attention, we often find ourselves wanting more. Just as often, we don't have the first idea about how to seek God on our own without the support of our small group.

Catholic tradition contains a treasure trove of spiritual riches on which to draw. This appendix offers a variety of means by which to come to know Jesus more deeply: discussing Scripture with a friend, reading the Bible, and reading the writings of the saints and spiritual teachers. Skim to find what appeals to your heart.

For a Discussion with a Christian Friend

Please read Hebrews 4:12 together and discuss the following questions:

1. What does the metaphor "sharper than any two-edged sword" mean to you?

2. Why would the word of God penetrate "soul and spirit, joints and marrow"? What do you think the writer of Hebrews wants you to understand by this image/metaphor?

3. Can you explain in practical terms how the word of God judges the reflections and thoughts of the heart?

4. Have you ever experienced the word of God becoming "living" to you, touching your heart and mind to convert you, even if it was about something minor?

5. Do you ever turn to the word of God in times when you don't have anywhere else to turn? What have been the results?

6. What challenges have you had with Scripture? How have you been able to work through them?

Getting to Know Christ through the Bible

1. A pen and paper can make the difference between reading the Bible and really meditating on it—considering the story or teaching deeply in order to become more familiar with Jesus.

2. Write down observations about the text as you read, and record questions that come to your mind, either in the margins of your Bible or in a journal.

3. Look up cross-references if your Bible has them, or look online, especially if they relate to your questions. Record your insights.

4. Find a key word in your text that interests you and use an online concordance to review where else it appears. Read those other passages to deepen your understanding of the meaning of that word. Note your feelings.

5. For those who are more visual, draw a picture inspired by a Scripture story.

6. Summarize in writing what happened in the Scripture passage you read, or what the writer was saying.

The Three Essentials for a Rich Experience of God through Scripture: Memorize, Meditate, and Apply

Memorize

We may think that memorization is tedious and a waste of time, but that's not true. Having the words of Jesus or his followers readily at hand can be an important step in getting to know him. When you really come to know a friend, you will sometimes think, "I know what 'Joe' would say in this situation." This is also the case with Jesus. As you come to know him better, you'll want to be able to recall something he has said, because as you do, you will feel his presence more intensely. But you can only do this if you have memorized his words.

If you know it by heart, Scripture is available to you anytime, anywhere, day or night, whether you are free or imprisoned, healthy or sick, walking with a friend, or sitting quietly before the Eucharist.

Here are some techniques to help you with memorization:

1. Memorizing is much more fruitful after you've meditated on a passage. (See instructions for meditation below.)

2. Memorize steadily for a few days rather than cramming all at once. You will retain the information longer, and meditating on it will give you time to consider what is being said.

3. Continue to review the words you have memorized, or you will lose them. One of the best times to do this is right before you

fall asleep. At bedtime you don't need the fresh mind necessary for new memorization.

Meditate

Meditation is deep thinking on the teachings and spiritual realities in Scripture for the purposes of understanding, application, and prayer. A short description could be "absorption," "focused attention," or "intense consideration."

Meditation goes beyond hearing, reading, studying, or even memorizing. Instead, it is a means of absorbing the words and allowing God to speak to you through them.

Both Jews and Christians have attested that *God uses Scripture to speak to us.* When we make ourselves available to God mentally and spiritually in this way, he will reach us through his word.

God is gentle and gracious—he will never force us. Rather, he continuously invites us. When we give the time and attention that meditation requires, God in return gives us all the gifts a loving father longs to give his children.

Start with verses that conspicuously relate to your own concerns and personal needs. These can be found easily on any Internet search engine. (For example, search "Scripture passages on anxiety" or "Bible verses on seeking God's strength.") Through Scripture verses relevant to your life, God can meet your needs very quickly. He wants our communication with Jesus to be rooted in the Scriptures.

Some tips and methods for meditation:

1. Summarize in your own words what the passage is saying, or what happens in what order in a narrative or dialogue.

- You can do this in your head, but it's even better if you jot it down in a journal. This is an extremely useful practice. Some of us think we know the Scriptures because they are proclaimed in church, particularly the Gospels. When we try to summarize in the order of events/dialogue, however, we learn how much we have been missing!

- Don't worry about trying to summarize from memory—you should go back to the text to clarify. Sometimes observing that you have glossed over verses can be an indication that you need to spend time on a particular teaching.

2. Talk to Jesus about the Scripture passage you are reading.

- By talking to Jesus, you submit your mind to the Holy Spirit's illumination of the text and intensify your spiritual perception.

- Allow time for both reading and talking to Jesus. If you rush through the reading, you won't retain anything. If you say a few words to Jesus and then dash off, you aren't really giving him time to speak or explain things to you. Think how much you retain or receive when you're rushed in speaking to another person. It's the same with God!

3. Don't bite off more than you can chew. Better to read and consider a few verses or a short passage than to ingest big chunks without meditation.

Apply

If we do something about what we have read, what we read is incorporated into our lives as it can be in no other way. "Be doers of the word, and not hearers only, deceiving yourselves" (James 1:22). An application is a concrete step you can take in response to your prayer and meditation.

1. Expect to find an application—open the Bible in anticipation of discovering what you need!

2. Meditate to discern an application. Meditation isn't an end in itself. It leads to inner transformation, and inner transformation comes from and leads to action.

3. Sometimes an action step is so evident that it jumps off the page. If this doesn't happen, be sure to ask questions of the text that orient you towards action. For example:

- Does this text reveal something I should believe?

- Does this text reveal something I should praise or thank or trust God for?

- Does this text reveal something I should pray about for myself and others?

- Does this text reveal something about which I should have a new attitude?

- Does this text reveal something about which I should make a decision?

- Does this text reveal something I should do for the sake of Christ and others or myself?

Commit to one specific response. Less is more if you really do it.

Scripture reading and meditation techniques are necessary because we all need to prevent shallow reading. Modern technology forms us for fast and superficial communication. In fact, we often talk to others shallowly because our attention is on texting, tweeting, the next thing we're doing—the list is endless!

We must fight this tendency for the sake of our humanity. In one episode of an old sci-fi television show, the original *Star Trek*, the former inhabitants of another planet had continually sped up, ultimately moving so fast that they became merely buzzing sounds. When they invaded the starship *Enterprise*, the crew thought that flies had come in with the food supplies. These aliens had lost their very beings because they valued speed above all else.

Watch to see if you're reading Scripture hurriedly or in a perfunctory way because you think you should, not because you are seeking to meet God there.

If Jesus met you on the street today, do you think he would be shallow, half listening, rushing, or distracted? Can these be the ways of a loving God? If not, then they can't be the way of a loving person either! Remember, Christ is those "other people" you will meet on the street and everywhere you go each day. Loving attention to God in Scripture forms us for loving attention to others.

Spiritual Reading

The Church has consistently valued the witness of the communion of saints. We are fortunate that as Catholics, we have a rich tradition of stories of holy men and women whose lives have witnessed to their great love of God and others. In addition, many saints canonized by the Church, as well as other spiritual teachers, have left written or artistic works that the Church recognizes as invaluable tools for coming to know God.

Perhaps—especially if you were raised Catholic—you already have an interest in a specific saint or spiritual teacher. If so, find out if that saint has left any written or artistic works. Either can be used to consider Jesus. Or ask a friend about saints whose writings have helped them. Biographies of the lives of saints and Christian heroes can also be inspiring reading.

Spiritual reading is much like Scripture meditation. If we read quickly and do not consider what we have read, nothing much sticks. If we read slowly and allow time to think about what we have read, then we absorb it. God communicates with us through considered reading.

Scripture reading with meditation holds priority over spiritual reading because Christians have always taught that the Scriptures are the privileged means by which God works in our hearts and minds. That is why Christians encourage daily reading of Scripture above any other spiritual reading. The saints and spiritual teachers enlighten and inspire us for the reading of Scripture.

The Evangelical Catholic recommends reading and meditating on Scripture in the morning, when you are fresh, or during a break in your day. You can save the spiritual reading for later on, either in the evening or at bedtime.

Writings of the Saints and Spiritual Teachers

Some classics that have helped those seeking to know Christ:

The Way of Perfection by Teresa of Avila. This is the best book to begin with when reading St. Teresa. A Doctor of the Church, Teresa is loved by many for her writings on prayer and the spiritual life. This book is short and simple. Teresa's direct language and folksy style make for a particularly engaging read.

Autobiography of Teresa of Avila, also called *The Story of Her Life.* This is longer than *The Way of Perfection* and includes St. Teresa's famous metaphor on prayer as a garden. Read this when you're ready for extended time with St. Teresa.

The Story of a Soul, also called *The Autobiography of St. Thérèse of Lisieux* . In surveys on favorite saints, St. Thérèse consistently tops the list. She speaks in her memoir with an unaffected, honest voice, almost like the voice of a child. She died as a cloistered Carmelite nun at the age of twenty-four, but despite her young age, she was soon recognized as a spiritual giant. St. Thérèse is known for her "little way" of humble love. For first-time readers, her little way may appear simple or silly. But once you try it, you learn that loving sacrificially, like Jesus, truly does require you to lose your life in order to save it.

Introduction to the Devout Life by St. Francis de Sales. This is a great read for beginners because it has so much direction on how to live as a follower of Jesus. You can read each short and accessible chapter in only ten to fifteen minutes. Reading one each day will give you plenty of real spiritual meat to chew on.

Pensées by Blaise Pascal. This classic has influenced countless Christians. Pascal was a seventeenth-century mathematician. The *pensées*, or "thoughts," are scattered fragments of his theological and philosophical ponderings after his conversion to Christianity.

New Seeds of Contemplation and *No Man Is an Island* by Thomas Merton. Merton is widely considered one of the greatest spiritual writers of the twentieth century. His compartmentalized prose provides quick, sophisticated reading "nuggets" capable of leading you into profound thoughts on God. The language of his later works is more accessible than those of his earlier ones.

The Confessions of Saint Augustine. This well-loved classic details Augustine's search for God. The immediacy of his struggle to believe is evident and something every person, even today, can relate to. Augustine's conversion story finishes with Book 9. The later chapters are written as a long disquisition on time and memory. This is rich stuff, but it's not for every reader.

The Imitation of Christ by Thomas à Kempis. Apart from the Bible, no book has been translated into more languages than this classic. It was a favorite of Teresa of Avila, Thomas More, Ignatius of Loyola (founder of the Jesuits), Thérèse of Lisieux, and countless saints and Christians of other denominations, including John Wesley and John Newton, founders of the Methodist movement. The book has remained popular because of its profound insights about human nature and the struggle to live a holy life.

Autobiography of Saint Ignatius of Loyola. This short description of St. Ignatius' famous conversion from a womanizing soldier to a Christian mendicant, or beggar, is both a classic and an easy read. The story includes Ignatius' observations on his interior life while convalescing from serious war wounds. These become not only the immediate cause of his conversion but also the groundwork for his thought on the discernment of spirits in his *Spiritual Exercises.*

The Long Loneliness by Dorothy Day. Day was a worldly young communist in the heyday of early twentieth-century social movements. She lived in New York City as many young women live today: taking lovers, having an abortion, and promoting a secular salvation through political change. After her conversion to Catholicism, Day founded the Catholic Worker movement, still in existence today, to offer hospitality to Christ in the poor and needy. Simply written and very moving, Day's is one of the great conversion stories of the last century.

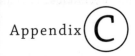

Appendix C

As we draw closer to the Lord, we begin to realize that he wants to speak to us. Here are some guidelines to help you as you learn to listen to God in prayer.

Begin by getting off your mind the things that you need and want, your sorrows, frustrations, and questions. Talk to God in your own words about anything on your mind or heart. Jesus tells us to do this (Luke 11:9-13). If we don't share our burdens with God, they keep "interrupting" us when we want to be quiet to listen.

After you've shared what's on your heart, tell Jesus that you give the rest of the time to him. Ask him to do with it as he pleases.

Say a simple prayer from your heart such as this one: "Jesus, I want to listen to you, hear you, and follow you. Bless this time."

Prayer techniques can be helpful, but in the end, your time with God is about your relationship with him. Sometimes we need to work at becoming better listeners with our friends and families. Especially in the early days of building a relationship, we listen a lot to learn more about our new friend. What is important to her? Does he laugh easily or prefer more serious conversation? What are her interests? What makes him happy, angry, sad, troubled, or frustrated?

We learn much of this sort of information about God from reading the Scriptures, especially through Jesus in the New Testament. When we approach Scripture prayerfully, God shows us his character, what he values, and how to live a godly life.

The Holy Spirit within us allows intimate connection with God. Even if we know almost nothing about the Scriptures, we can converse with God. But learning about the word and allowing God to speak to us through it should be every Christian's starting place for listening to the Lord.

Some people feel frustrated because they want specific directions from God about what to do. Very often, however, God doesn't give us such instructions. He wants to form our hearts so that we can make our own choices. God honors the freedom he has given us: he wants us to choose our own paths, but he wants us to choose in his light and love. This is how we become true to ourselves, the person he intended us to be when he created us in our mother's womb (cf. Psalm 139:13).

If God doesn't seem to be responding, try talking to God about his favorite subjects. Ask him if there is someone in your life he would like to bless in some way. If you don't know how to bless that person, ask God. Or ask him how to improve a relationship in your life. God very commonly responds to questions like these, and he makes his answers unmistakable!

When you've heard something from God, then do what God tells you. The more you obey, the more you will hear God speaking to you the next time. You will be a disciple he can rely on to take his love and mercy into the world.

Some Listening Prayer Methods

Find a quiet place where you can sit uninterrupted for fifteen to twenty minutes. Try to sit in a comfortable chair so that you're not distracted physically. You can kneel if you wish, although you may find it difficult to be in that position the entire time. Listening in prayer is not usually an ascetical practice, although occasionally you may feel called to kneel or lie prostrate on the floor, especially during Lent or at other times of penitence.

All of the things that helped you listen in school will help you attend to God. Sit up straight with both feet on the floor. Don't slouch or lie down.

Then take a few deep breaths to clear your mind. The Hebrew word for "spirit" in the Scriptures is *ruah*, meaning breath or wind. Breathe in and out, knowing that the Holy Spirit—holy breath—is with you, giving you life.

Quiet your mind as much as possible, and look into the darkness of your closed eyes. Some people find it helpful to focus on the inside of their eyelids or up toward their foreheads. Others visualize the Sacred Heart of Jesus, and then imagine moving into his heart.

Another method is to imagine your brain having layers like an onion, with a surface layer—always busy thinking, worrying, fantasizing, planning, remembering—and a deeper, darker, more obscure part. Visualize moving into that deepest, darkest part. Try to rest quietly in God.

Ask God your questions, share your concerns, and then rest quietly in the Lord. When you find yourself thinking of other things—which you will, because that is how the human mind works—just turn your thoughts back to God and focus on Jesus. You may not feel his presence, but believe what he has promised: "I am with you always, even until the end of time" (cf. Matthew 28:20). On faith, believe he is with you, because he is! ("Faith is the assurance of things hoped for, the conviction of things not seen" [Hebrews 11:1].) When you notice yourself thinking of something, gently, without rebuke, return to any visualization or prayer that you were using to quiet your mind.

Never condemn yourself because you experience distractions. In her masterpiece on prayer, *Interior Castle*, St. Teresa of Avila said she made a wonderful discovery: God was working in her whether she thought of something else during prayer or not.[1] How great is our God! Have faith that God wants intimacy with you, and will carve out the space within you in which his Holy Spirit will dwell, just because you're *trying* to pray. Failure is impossible if you just try!

Some people find sitting still too stifling. If you feel this way, take a walk in a pleasant environment such as a park or the woods. Busy city streets usually don't work—there is too much bustle and distraction. Jesus said to go into your "room" (Matthew 6:6), or "secret place," to pray. This could be interpreted metaphorically. If you can focus your mind while walking, that can be your secret place. If you can't focus, take Jesus literally: go to your room and close the door.

(Note to extreme extroverts or those with attention deficit disorders: walking is probably not the method for you. Because of the visual stimulation and distractions, you would probably struggle to keep your attention on God.)

Whether you sit or walk, as you begin, be clear in your thoughts that you are giving this time to God. A walk can't be an ordinary walk and be prayer. We can't sit in our rooms daydreaming the whole time without making an effort to pray.

Some people find it helpful to visualize Christ beside them. If you are walking, you could picture Jesus as though he were walking with you. Some visualize the Holy Spirit floating along above them. Come up with your own visualization, or don't use one if it isn't helpful.

Whether sitting or walking, allow times when you are quiet instead of talking to God. Sometimes God replies through the Holy Spirit right away. Other times, after our prayer time, an answer, an idea, or a direction in the form of a thought will come very clearly into your mind. That's God speaking to you!

People who feel burdened by racing, distracted, or otherwise unfocused minds often write down their conversations with God in a journal. This makes possible more focus and less distraction than almost any other prayer method. Once you have established a prayerful disposition, write down your concerns and questions to God. The writing can help move you into a quiet place in which God can guide you in writing—and even in writing his responses to you! Many praying people who journal say they are able to start distinguishing very quickly, in a few weeks' time, what comes from them in writing and what comes from God.

At the end of the time you've allocated for prayer, always thank God for the ways in which he has worked in you. Ask him to support any resolutions you have made. Close with the Our Father.

[1]"Just as we cannot stop the movement of the heavens, revolving as they do with such speed, so we cannot restrain our thought. And then we send all the faculties of the soul after it, thinking we are lost, and have misused the time that we are spending in the presence of God. Yet the soul may perhaps be wholly united with Him in the Mansions very near His presence, while thought remains in the outskirts of the castle, suffering the assaults of a thousand wild and venomous creatures and from this suffering winning merit. So this must not upset us, and we must not abandon the struggle, as the devil tries to make us do." Reprinted from *Interior Castle* by St. Teresa of Avila, trans. and ed. E. Allison Peers (New York: Doubleday), 1972, p. 58.

Appendix  D

Forgiveness is a response of mercy and love to an injustice. If we fail to forgive, the lack of forgiveness festers.

The Catholic philosopher Dietrich von Hildebrand ranked resentment alongside hatred as a "poisonous" inner state.[1] To clear out the poison of resentment, first examine your conscience to see if the things you resent are important or petty.

If you're given to taking offense easily and over small matters, you may find that the problem isn't with those you think have wronged you; the problem is with you! Ask God daily this week to help change your temperament, to make you more meek and humble so that you are less sensitive to slights. Try to forgive one specific small slight, and note how that affects your interior life. If your resentment arises from someone truly hurting you or treating you unjustly, forgiveness can free you of the inner poison.

To begin forgiving, we need to know what forgiveness is not; otherwise we will seek what cannot be found. Forgiveness is not forgetting, denying, condoning, or excusing the injustice. It is not condemning the offender, nor does it involve a sense of moral superiority over the one who wronged you. It is an act of mercy that is different than seeking justice, but the two are not mutually exclusive.

Ideally, we practice the virtues of forgiveness and justice simultaneously. For example, if someone intentionally damaged your property, you can forgive that person and ask for compensation. Virtues are not meant to be practiced in isolation.

However, the inability to secure justice concurrently does not justify resentment or other forms of unforgiveness, and neither does it make them less poisonous. Resentment is still spiritual venom, and a lack of forgiveness binds us whether justice can be had or not.

Reconciliation and healing of relationships is one of the goals of forgiveness, but forgiveness is not the same as reconciliation. If it is not possible or safe to reconcile with the person who has hurt you, you can still forgive without ever achieving reconciliation.

The exercise that follows has been adapted from Dr. Robert D. Enright's five-part lecture series, "Healing Through Forgiveness: Making Our Way to Good Friday and Easter Resurrection." You may also want to read his book, *Forgiveness Is a Choice*.[2] Another excellent resource is *Blessing Your Enemies, Forgiving Your Friends: A Scriptural Journey into Personal Peace* by Kristen Johnson Ingram.[3]

It may take you a week, a month, a year, or even longer to work through the forgiveness process. Take your time and record your progress in a journal.

Christ could heal you completely through this spiritual exercise, or you may need further assistance. Many books and spiritual guides teach different ways to work through the process of forgiveness. Find one that helps you.

Preliminaries: Unity with Jesus

Forgiveness is an intimate encounter with Jesus Christ in his passion and resurrection. It is painful to forgive someone who has hurt you and to love that person anyway when he or she doesn't seem to deserve it. Yet the process is freeing and healing. When we forgive, we walk the path of the cross and journey toward the resurrection.

The process involves suffering, but we are not alone. Jesus has been through it all before. He knows how to navigate through the pain. Without a close relationship with Jesus, you will not be able to forgive to the depth that only he makes possible. Jesus said, "Apart from me you can do nothing" (John 15:5). His words apply to all things, including forgiveness.

Pray for unity with Jesus before you begin this process of forgiveness, and throughout your efforts as well. Ask Jesus to come into your heart, to dwell there, and to enkindle within you the fire of his love. Let Jesus guide you on the road to forgiveness.

The Process of Forgiveness

Who hurt you? On which specific incident will you focus?

Pick one person who unjustly hurt you and where you still feel hurt. This person may have hurt you numerous times, but for now focus on one specific incident that still stirs up your heart. If you are not sure which event to choose, ask Jesus to help you.

What were the specific circumstances at the time? How deeply were you hurt?

Remember the details of the incident. Was it morning or afternoon? Cloudy or sunny? What was said? How did you respond at the time? How did you respond across time up to the present? What pierced your heart most about the incident? Can you describe and name your hurt? Did you feel shame, humiliation, or betrayal? How deep is your wound? Rate your pain on a scale of one to ten, ten being pain that barely allows you to function. Don't be ashamed at the level of your pain. You didn't deserve the injustice, and you have a right to be upset about it.

Phase 1: Uncovering your Anger and Suffering

We often cover up our anger or suffering so that we don't have to deal with it. If we don't face the pain, however, we won't heal. Try to think about all the different ways in which the offense has caused you suffering. Many layers of pain probably need to be uncovered and examined, and every layer is another level of suffering from the offense that you didn't deserve.

The following questions will help you to reflect on the layers of pain the injustice has left you. Ask the Holy Spirit to help you understand the level of anger you have over the offense.

- Have you faced your anger or suffering?
- Are you afraid to expose your shame or guilt?
- Have you used diversions to avoid dealing with your anger or suffering?
- Has your anger affected your health?
- Have you lost energy?
- Have you been obsessed about the injury or the offender?
- Do you compare your situation with that of the offender?
- Has the injury caused a change in your life?
- Did the injury distort the shape of your life?
- Has the injury formed or changed your worldview?

Phase 2: Deciding to Forgive

You don't have to feel like forgiving to begin forgiving. You can simply decide to begin. Be willing to continue the process, and make a commitment to work on it.

One of the strongest motivations for starting to forgive is all the pain that refusing to forgive causes you and all the energy that cherishing the wrong requires. Forgiveness is not about you alone, but your motivation initially might be that the failure to forgive causes you suffering.

Phase 3: Working on Forgiveness

Work toward understanding.

After you are very clear about the wrong you have suffered and how it has affected your life and you make the decision that you want to forgive, the next step is to work toward understanding the person who hurt you. Try to understand him or her as another human being.

- What were the circumstances of his or her life before they hurt you?
- How did he or she grow up?
- What is his or her life like now?

Work toward compassion.

As you gain a greater understanding of the person who hurt you and the circumstances of his or her life, work on caring about that person. It is likely that he or she, too, is wounded. Caring will feel challenging because it seems as if he or she does not or did not care about you. Understanding his or her woundedness can soften your heart.

Imagine you and the person who hurt you both at the foot of the cross, both in need of redemption. Try to see him or her as a child of God, deserving of God's mercy, just as you are. Jesus died for both of you.

If your heart begins to soften for that person, you are feeling compassion. Ask the Holy Spirit to cultivate that feeling, and hold it in your heart.

As you reflect on these things, do not make light of the offense. What the person did to you was wrong, *and yet,* he or she is a beloved child of God, just as you are, even though you sometimes do wrong. According to justice, that person doesn't deserve kindness from you. According to God's mercy, he or she deserves kindness, respect, and love.

Accept the pain.

Next, accept the pain you feel as a result of the injustice. When we ignore the pain, we tend to displace it onto others in various ways. If you bear the pain, you will avoid spreading the hurt.

As you try to bear your pain, unite your pain with Jesus' on the cross. Jesus is also wounded, and he shares your wound. Unite your wound with Christ's wounds. Try to look at the person who hurt you with love from the cross. Crucified with Christ, you are beginning to love as he loves.

Give the offender a gift.

Give the one who hurt you a gift. Remember, while we were still sinners, Christ died for us (Romans 5:8). He didn't care that we were, and are, inclined to sin.

What kind of gift can you give the one who hurt you? Maybe it's not wise or possible to reestablish the relationship. But if it is, and if you haven't spoken to the person in a while, a card or a call might work. Perhaps the gift you could give the person is something as simple as a smile or saying a prayer for him or her. If the one who hurt you is deceased, you might have a Mass said for the person or speak about the person positively.

It can cause another wound to reach out to the one who hurt you, but with Christ you are touching that person's wounded heart and becoming a conduit of healing for him or her.

Phase 4: Discovery and Release from Emotional Prison

Walking the path of forgiveness is walking the path of the cross with Christ. It's a road up a mountain bearing the injury and insult, carrying the heavy cross that presses on painful open wounds.

Christ no doubt wanted his own way of the cross to be shorter and quicker than it was. Forgiveness takes time. We take a few steps forward, our cross seems lighter, and then unexpectedly the weight returns, as heavy and painful as it ever was.

But over time, we can see that we are making progress. We think of the wrong less often; we have more hope, more peace. Slowly the wrong loses its power over us.

Talking to a priest, pastoral minister, or trusted Christian friend can be tremendously helpful as you walk the way of Jesus. The apostle John, his mother, Mary, and several women disciples stood at the foot of the cross during Jesus' crucifixion. They probably walked the whole painful road up to Calvary.

If you don't know whom to ask to walk with you through this difficult journey, ask Jesus to tell you or to bring someone into your life who can help you.

"For freedom Christ has set you free" (cf. Galatians 5:1). The way of forgiveness doesn't end on Calvary. The healing that comes from forgiveness gives us a foretaste of the full freedom that the glory of the resurrection makes possible, and that will one day be yours.

[1]"Rancor . . . and similar experiences of resentment are always likely . . . to injure the freedom of the soul. . . . In order to stay in the soft, gentle, open attitude of loving-kindness, we must, above all, constantly elevate our eyes to the face of the divine Savior. . . . In fact we should aim at dwelling in that light so permanently that our very first awareness of an injustice or a slight inflicted upon us will already be impregnated with the spirit of meekness and free from any trace of the poison of resentment." Reprinted from Dietrich von Hildebrand, *Transformation in Christ: On Christian Attitude* (San Francisco: Ignatius Press), 2001, pp. 281, 415–416.
[2]Robert D. Enright, PhD, *Forgiveness Is a Choice: A Step-by-Step Process for Resolving Anger and Restoring Hope* (Washington, DC: American Psychological Association), 2001.
[3]Kristen Johnson Ingram, *Blessing Your Enemies, Forgiving Your Friends: A Scriptural Journey into Personal Peace* St. Louis, MO: Liguori Publications), 1993.

Appendix

If it has been a long time since you last went to Confession—or if you've never been—you may be hesitant and unsure. Don't let these very common feelings get in your way. Reconciling with God and the Church always brings great joy. Take the plunge—you will be glad you did!

If it will help to alleviate your fears, familiarize yourself with the step-by-step description of the process below. Most priests are happy to help anyone willing to take the risk. If you forget anything, the priest will remind you. So don't worry about committing every step and word to memory. Remember, Jesus isn't giving you a test; he just wants you to experience the grace of his mercy!

Catholics believe that the priest acts *in persona Christi,* "in the person of Christ." The beauty of the sacraments is that they touch us both physically and spiritually. On the physical level in Confession, we hear the words of absolution through the person of the priest. On the spiritual level, we know that it is Christ assuring us that he has truly forgiven us. We are made clean!

You usually have the option of going to Confession anonymously—in a confessional booth or in a room with a screen—or face-to-face with the priest. Whatever your preference will be fine with the priest.

Steps in the Sacrament of Reconciliation:

1. Prepare to receive the sacrament by praying and examining your conscience. If you need help, you can find

many different lists of questions online that will help you examine your conscience.

2. Once you're with the priest, begin by making the Sign of the Cross while greeting the priest with these words: "Bless me, Father, for I have sinned." Then tell him how long it has been since your last confession. If it's your first confession, tell him so.

3. Confess your sins to the priest. If you are unsure about anything, ask him to help you. Place your trust in God, who is a merciful and loving Father.

4. When you are finished, indicate this by saying, "I am sorry for these and all of my sins." Don't worry later that you forgot something. This closing statement covers everything that didn't come to mind in the moment. Trust God that he has brought to mind what he wanted you to address.

5. The priest will assign you a penance, such as a prayer, a Scripture reading, or a work of mercy, service, or sacrifice.

6. Express sorrow for your sins by saying an Act of Contrition. Many versions of these prayers can be found online. If memorization is difficult for you, just say you're sorry in your own words.

7. The priest, acting again in the person of Christ, will absolve you of your sins with prayerful words, ending with, "I absolve you from your sins in the name of the Father, and of the Son, and of the Holy Spirit." You respond by making the Sign of the Cross and saying, "Amen."

8. The priest will offer some proclamation of praise, such as "Give thanks to the Lord, for he is good" (from Psalm 136). You can respond, "His mercy endures forever."

9. The priest will dismiss you.

10. Be sure to complete your assigned penance immediately or as soon as possible.

According to the *Catechism of the Catholic Church*, an examination of conscience is a "prayerful self-reflection on our words and deeds in the light of the Gospel to determine how we may have sinned against God" (Glossary). You can access guides to help you in that process at the website of the United States Conference of Catholic Bishops at http://www.usccb.org/prayer-and-worship/sacraments-and-sacramentals/penance/examinations-of-conscience.cfm.

Appendices for Facilitators

(F) The Role of a Facilitator

(G) A Guide for Each Session of *With Jesus to the Cross: Year C*

(H) Leading Prayer and "Connection to the Cross This Week"

Appendix (F)

Perhaps no skill is more important to the success of a small group than the ability to facilitate a discussion lovingly. It is God's Holy Spirit working through our personal spiritual journey, not necessarily our theological knowledge, that makes this possible.

The following guidelines can help facilitators avoid some of the common pitfalls of small group discussion. The goal is to open the door for the Spirit to take the lead and guide your every response because you are attuned to his movements.

Pray daily and before your small group meeting. This is the only way you can learn to sense the Spirit's gentle promptings when they come!

You are a Facilitator, Not a Teacher

As a facilitator, it can be extremely tempting to answer every question. You may have excellent answers and be excited about sharing them with your brothers and sisters in Christ. However, a more Socratic method, by which you attempt to draw answers from participants, is much more fruitful for everyone else and for you as well.

Get in the habit of reflecting participants' questions or comments to the whole group before offering your own input. It is not necessary for you as a facilitator to enter immediately into the discussion or to offer a magisterial answer. When others have sufficiently addressed an issue, try to exercise restraint in your comments. Simply affirm what has been said; then thank them and move on.

If you don't know the answer to a question, have a participant look it up in the *Catechism of the Catholic Church* and read it aloud to the group. If you cannot find an answer, ask someone to research the question for the next session. Never feel embarrassed to say, "I don't know." Simply acknowledge the quality of the question and offer to follow up with that person after you have done some digging. Remember, you are a facilitator, not a teacher.

Affirm and Encourage

We are more likely to repeat a behavior when it is openly encouraged. If you want more active participation and sharing, give positive affirmation to the responses of the group members. This is especially important if people are sharing from their hearts. A simple "Thank you for sharing that" can go a long way in encouraging further discussion in your small group.

If someone has offered a theologically questionable response, don't be nervous or combative. Wait until others have offered their input. It is very likely that someone will proffer a more helpful response, which you can affirm by saying something such as, "That is the Christian perspective on that topic. Thank you."

If no acceptable response is given and you know the answer, exercise great care and respect in your comments so as not to appear smug or self-righteous. You might begin with something such as, "Those are all interesting perspectives. What the Church has said about this is . . . "

Avoid Unhelpful Tangents

Nothing can derail a Spirit-filled discussion more quickly than digressing on unnecessary tangents. Try to keep the session on track. If conversation strays from the topic, ask yourself, "Is this a

Spirit-guided tangent?" Ask the Holy Spirit too! If not, bring the group back by asking a question that steers conversation to the Scripture passage or to a question you have been discussing. You may even suggest kindly, "Have we gotten a little off topic?" Most participants will respond positively and get back on track through your sensitive leading.

That being said, some tangents may be worth pursuing if you sense a movement of the Spirit. It may be exactly where God wants to steer the discussion. You will find that taking risks can yield some beautiful results.

Don't Fear the Silence

Be okay with silence. Most people need a moment or two to come up with a response to a question. People naturally require some time to formulate their thoughts and put them into words. Some may need a few moments just to gather the courage to speak at all.

Regardless of the reason, don't be afraid of a brief moment of silence after asking a question. Let everyone in the group know early on that silence is an integral part of normal small group discussion. They needn't be anxious or uncomfortable when it happens. God works in silence!

This applies to times of prayer as well. If no one shares or prays after a sufficient amount of time, just move on gracefully.

The Power of Hospitality

A little hospitality can go far in creating community. Everybody likes to feel cared for. This is especially true in a small group whose purpose it is to connect to Jesus Christ, a model for care, support, and compassion.

Make a point to greet people personally when they first arrive. Ask them how their day has been going. Take some time to invest in the lives of your small group participants. Pay particular attention to newcomers. Work at remembering each person's name. Help everyone feel comfortable and at home. Allow your small group to be an environment where authentic relationships take shape and blossom.

Encourage Participation

Help everyone to get involved, especially those who are naturally less vocal or outgoing. To encourage participation initially, always invite various group members to read aloud the selected readings. Down the road, even after the majority of the group feels comfortable sharing, you may still have some quieter members who rarely volunteer a response to a question but would be happy to read.

Meteorology?

Keep an eye on the "Holy Spirit barometer." Is the discussion pleasing to the Holy Spirit? Is this conversation leading participants to a deeper personal connection to Jesus Christ? The intellectual aspects of our faith are certainly important to discuss, but conversation can sometimes degenerate into an unedifying showcase of intellect and ego. Other times discussion becomes an opportunity for gossip, detraction, complaining, or even slander. When this happens, you can almost feel the Holy Spirit leaving the room!

If you are aware that this dynamic has taken over a discussion, take a moment to pray quietly in your heart. Ask the Holy Spirit to help you bring the conversation to a more wholesome topic. This can often be achieved simply by moving to the next question.

Pace

Generally, you want to pace the session to finish in the allotted time, but sometimes this may be impossible without sacrificing quality discussion. If you reach the end of your meeting and find that you have covered only half the material, don't fret! This is often the result of lively Spirit-filled discussion and meaningful theological reflection.

In such a case, you may take time at another meeting to cover the remainder of the material. If you only have a small portion left, you can ask participants to pray through these on their own and come to the following meeting with any questions or insights they might have. Even if you must skip a section to end on time, make sure you leave adequate time for prayer and to review the "Connection to the Cross This Week" section. This is vital in helping participants integrate their discoveries from the group into their daily lives.

Genuine Friendships

The best way to show Jesus' love for and interest in your small group members is to meet with them for coffee, dessert, or a meal outside of your small group time.

You can begin by suggesting that the whole group get together for ice cream or some other social event at a different time than when your small group usually meets. Socializing will allow relationships to develop. It provides the opportunity for different kinds of conversations than small group sessions allow. You will notice an immediate difference in the quality of community in your small group at the next meeting.

After that first group social, try to meet one-on-one with each person in your small group. This allows for more in-depth conversation and personal sharing, giving you the chance to know each participant better so that you can love and care for them as Jesus would.

Jesus called the twelve apostles in order that they could "be with him" (Mark 3:14). When people spend time together, eat together, laugh together, cry together, and talk about what matters to them, intense Christian community develops. That is the kind of community Jesus was trying to create, and that must be the kind of community we try to create, because it changes lives. And changed lives change the world!

Joy

Remember that seeking the face of the Lord brings joy! Nothing is more fulfilling, more illuminating, and more beautiful than fostering a deep and enduring relationship with Jesus Christ. Embrace your participants and the entire spiritual journey with a spirit of joyful anticipation of what God wants to accomplish.

> "These things I have spoken to you, that my joy may be in you, and that your joy may be full." (John 15:11)

Appendix (G)

The following notes will help you be better prepared to facilitate each session. They include suggestions for helping people become comfortable with the group, for dealing with sensitive topics, for learning to pray aloud together, and for celebrating the resurrection together. Review the notes for each session as you prepare each week.

Week 1
Hope in the Desert

In this first meeting, spend a few minutes facilitating introductions. Ask people to introduce themselves and share one other thing about themselves. Set a time limit of a minute or two so that this doesn't consume too much time.

The tone of the question should be light. For example, asking them about their favorite part of the Lenten season would be better than asking them why they came to the group. The question need not be religious: it can be about favorite sports teams or players, favorite movies or books and why, and so forth. Avoid anything deeply personal. Your goal is to help people become comfortable before plunging into more substantive discussion.

As the group facilitator, you should lead the opening prayer to set a prayerful tone. In future meetings, you could ask a group member to lead the prayer.

The opening prayer asks the leader to pause. Since this is the first meeting, you will not be able to pause very long without causing discomfort, but try to have at least thirty seconds of silence.

When you review the "Connection to the Cross This Week" exercise as a group, strongly encourage members to memorize one of the Scripture verses during the upcoming week. It could be helpful to discuss what obstacles might prevent them from memorizing a short passage. Afterward, without objecting to people's concerns, you might exhort the group to make an effort to pray for one another to be able to memorize a Scripture verse. It would be ideal if you could testify to the power of this spiritual discipline in your own life.

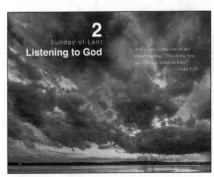

Week 2
Listening to God

After the opening prayer, you may want to ask participants about their experience of memorizing Scripture during the last week. Take care not to make group members feel guilty if they did not do this. To encourage people, give them a chance to share their struggles as well as the spiritual rewards they may have experienced.

The Gospel this week describes the transfiguration, when Peter, James, and John saw Moses and Elijah with Jesus glorified on the mountaintop.

Though no questions on the Scripture passage pertain to this, it may be helpful for you to know that traditionally the Church has interpreted this story as a "theophany," a revelation of God. The presence of Moses and Elijah shows Jesus' tie to both the law, given on Mount Sinai to Moses, and the prophets, through whom God spoke in ages past.

When you come to the "Connection to the Cross This Week" section, you probably won't have time to review all the day-to-day instructions in "Content for Listening Conversations with God." Just review the introductory section, and encourage participants to try at least some of the exercises so that the group can talk about their experiences together next week.

Week 3
The Fruit of Freedom

By this time, the group might be sufficiently comfortable for you to ask someone else to lead the opening prayer. If you do this, ask someone in advance so that they have time to prepare. You can begin to equip future leaders by sharing the responsibility!

After the opening prayer, ask how people have experienced the exercises to listen to God. This could launch a lengthy discussion full of excitement and/or discouragement. Rejoice with those who felt they heard from God, and encourage those who didn't by saying something such as this: "God has his own ways of communicating with each one of us. Sometimes it happens quickly, sometimes slowly. God always does what is best for each one of us. Keep pressing into prayer so that you can find the way God communicates with you."

Question number 2, the first question on the reading from Exodus, is meant to elicit a general summary to ground the conversation in salvation history. Some people may not be aware of the situation. You don't need to seek an elaborate explanation. Something such as this would be fine: "The Israelites were enslaved in Egypt. They went there when there was a famine in their own land. Later Pharoah enslaved them." If people don't seem to know this story, you should tell it!

The closing prayer is short so that you have time to lead the group in extemporaneous prayer first. A written prayer can never sum up the ways in which God has moved your conversation and hearts during the meeting, or express your hopes and fears. See Appendix H for ideas about how to help people become comfortable talking together to God aloud in their own words.

Week 4
Embracing
Forgiveness

The readings and discussion this week touch on emotionally tender territory: hurts and wrongs we have suffered, hurts and wrongs we have dealt to others. You will need to handle all the questions very carefully and allow more time and space for people to respond.

One way to couch questions gently is to begin with a phrase we have added to many of the questions in this session.

- "Would anyone feel comfortable sharing about . . . ?"

- "No pressure if you're not comfortable, but could anyone talk in general terms about a time someone wronged you and your response . . . ?"

Then allow plenty of quiet time. Participants need that time to gather their thoughts and figure out a way to describe their situation without revealing more than they are comfortable sharing. As you ask each delicate question, pray that the Holy Spirit will both prompt group members to share their experiences and help them find the right way to do it.

If group members do not open up, you cannot and should not try to force it. Sometimes sharing a personal experience yourself helps others to be more comfortable sharing theirs. Prepare something in advance about a time that you were hurt and had to forgive. Frame it in a way that will be comfortable for you. This will model how to speak in generalities rather than being too specific about details.

Sometimes conversations about forgiveness can lead to tears or other expressions of sorrow. They may also stir up old anger. When this happens, it shows that group members have grown to trust one another. Don't hasten past the surfacing of these deep feelings. A few seconds of silence allows time for the power of what was said to sink into everyone's hearts. Honor the person by thanking him or her for sharing this burden of their heart.

Ask the person if the group could pray for him or her right then and there. It can be powerfully comforting when members of the group lay hands on the person's shoulders or arms while praying.

Fully transition from any emotions that need tending to before reviewing "Connection to the Cross This Week," which suggests participants seek the Sacrament of Reconciliation during the coming week. This is important because you don't want people to feel that you're suggesting that the way to address the wrongs done to them is to confess the injuries they've done to others.

"If any one is in Christ, he is a new creation" (2 Corinthians 5:17). This phrase from the second reading, one of the most famous of St. Paul's, can help you minister to difficult emotions if they arise in your conversation. After a time of discussion and possibly prayer for someone, you could talk about how forgiveness helps us to become the "new creations" St. Paul says we are instead of being imprisoned in our wounds and brokenness. Then refer the group to Appendix D. Explain that it offers help for those ready to work toward forgiving someone. This can help create a clean segue to reviewing the suggestion about Confession in "Connection to the Cross This Week."

As you review, show people that Appendex E provides guidance for the Sacrament of Reconciliation.

Any personal witness you can give to the power of this sacrament in your own life can help inspire those who feel timid or fearful about telling their sins to a priest. Unfortunately, many Catholics rarely or never partake of this sacrament.

Week 5
Press On Toward the Goal

Because Confession can be a very private matter, you may wish to skip asking about their experience in the last week with "Connection to the Cross." On the other hand, the sacrament can be so powerfully healing that someone might have a beautiful testimony to share. You could ask a less specific question such as, "Did anyone experience any spiritual fruit/riches/victories in the last week that they'd like to share?"

Question 8 asks if anyone would be willing to share about a sin they have struggled to leave behind. Again, this is delicate territory. Before the meeting, prepare something of your own to share that discusses your struggle in a general way, without necessarily naming the sin. This will model for others that it is possible to discuss our spiritual battles in the group without divulging personal details.

When you review the "Connection to the Cross This Week" section as a group, you may want to have a handout prepared that provides the actual Scripture passages instead of just the citations. This will allow people to quickly review them and see which one strikes them. If participants commit to memorizing a passage while they are still together in the group, it's more likely they will actually do it before the next session.

Week 6
Jesus, Remember Me

You will not be able to spend much or any time at this meeting reviewing people's experience with memorizing Scripture during the last week. Reading the passion and discussing it will take too long.

This week your focus will be on helping the group experience more fully the great solemn mysteries of our faith: the death and resurrection of Jesus. Although you don't have to be overly emotional during the reading of the Scripture passages, try to keep a respectful tone, and a reverent one at critical moments such as Jesus' death.

Questions 14 and 15 ask the group members to imagine themselves as Judas. Read the paragraph that precedes these questions rather than asking someone else to do so in order to set the right tone. Here are some tips:

- Pray before you begin, asking the Holy Spirit to give you the right voice, timbre, and speed.
- Read the passage seriously, but not in an overly theatrical way that draws attention to yourself.
- Slower is always better with proclamation. It takes people time to hear and assimilate even familiar text.
- Allow a significant silent pause after reading the paragraph before you ask the questions. To help group members remain in the spirit of the reading, don't suggest that they open their eyes until after you've asked question 14.

- If no one responds immediately, allow a significant silent pause to elicit a response.

If you ask someone to read the Scripture passage describing Jesus' death (Luke 24:44-48), as the guide suggests, encourage that person to allow at least one full minute of silence where indicated. Explain to the group members that during this time, they should close their eyes and keep their minds focused, to the best of their ability, on Jesus' suffering and death. They may also kneel if they wish.

Because the readings are long, you may not have time to review the upcoming "Connection to the Cross This Week." If this is the case, encourage the participants to read through it on their own. Tell them that it is meant to inspire their Holy Week by recapping all that was discussed during the last five weeks.

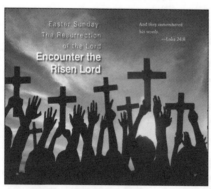

Week 7
Encounter the Risen Lord

Allow the joy of the resurrection to flow into your small group this week. The sacrifices of Lent should lead to a more joy-filled Easter! While the suffering in our lives probably isn't over, it takes on added meaning and dimension because Jesus' suffering overcame death. We are "more than conquerors through him who loved us" (Romans 8:37). Recognize that *all of reality* is renewed. Greet one another with this ancient Easter exchange: "He is risen!" "He is risen indeed!" After the discussion, rejoice together with special treats, sparkling juice, or even champagne. In whatever way feels appropriate, celebrate!

Be sure to allow time to review "Connection to the Cross This Year." Encourage people to take some of the suggestions in the "Living the Joy of the Resurrection throughout the Year" section into their daily lives. These practices will help the seeds planted during the Lenten small group take root rather than fall on rocky ground where no fruit can be born. Our daily relationship with the Lord in prayer and Scripture makes our hearts into "good soil," able to produce a harvest of thirty, sixty, and even a hundredfold (Mark 4:1-9).

Appendix

Opening Prayer

We have purposely provided a guided opening prayer for most sessions because it can help people who are completely new to small groups and shared prayer feel more at ease. If everyone or most people present are already comfortable with group prayer, involve them during subsequent gatherings.

As a facilitator, your goal is to provide opportunities for everyone to grow in leading prayer. After the first meeting, tell the group that you will allow time at the end of your prayer for others to voice their hopes for the group's time together. By Week 3, you could invite other people to open the group with prayer instead of using the prayer provided.

If you are comfortable leading an extemporaneous opening prayer, feel free to do that as soon as you wish. This would be ideal since some people have never witnessed spontaneous prayer. Such prayer demonstrates how to talk to God from the heart; it also expands the group's understanding of who God is and the relationship we can have with Jesus Christ.

You could begin any week by praising and thanking the Lord for the gift of gathering together. Thank God for giving each person present the desire to sacrifice their time to attend the group. You could ask the Holy Spirit to open hearts, illuminate minds, and deepen each person's experience of Lent through the Scripture passages you'll be reading. Ask the Holy Spirit to guide the discussion so that you can all grow from it. Close by saying something such as, "We pray this through Christ our Lord" or "We pray this in Jesus' name," and then end with the Sign of the Cross.

Some essentials for extemporaneous prayer:

- Speak in the first-person plural "we." For example, "Holy Spirit, we ask you to open our hearts . . . " It's fine to add a line asking the Holy Spirit to help you facilitate the discussion as he wills, or something else to that effect, but most of the prayer should be for the whole group.

- Model speaking directly to Jesus our Lord. This may sound obvious, but among Catholic laypeople, it isn't frequently practiced or modeled. This is a very evangelical thing to do in the sense that it witnesses to the gospel. Not only does it show how much the Lord loves us, but it also demonstrates our confidence that he listens to us. As we say our Lord's name, we remind ourselves, as well as those who hear us, that we aren't just talking to ourselves. This builds up our faith. Those unaccustomed to hearing someone pray in this way may feel a bit uncomfortable at first, but they will quickly become more at ease as they hear such prayers repeatedly. Remember, many graces come from praying "the name which is above every other name" (cf. Philippians 2:9). If you've never publicly prayed to Jesus, you may feel childish at first, but pray for the humility of a child. After all, Jesus said that we needed to become like children (Matthew 18:3)! The more we pray directly to Jesus in our personal prayer, the less awkward it will feel when we pray to him publicly.

- Model great faith and trust that the Lord hears your prayer and will answer it. It's terrific just to say in prayer, "Jesus, we trust you!"

- Extemporaneous prayer can be closed by inviting all to join in a prayer of the Church, such as the Glory Be, the Our Father, or the Hail Mary. This will bring all into the prayer.

Closing Prayer

For the closing prayer, we recommend that you include extemporaneous prayer, even if you also use the prayer provided. No written prayer can address the thoughts, concerns, feelings, and inspirations that come up during the discussion.

If some group members already feel comfortable praying aloud in their own words, invite the group to join in the closing prayer right away. If not, wait another week or two.

Once you feel that the group has the familiarity to prevent this from being too awkward, invite them to participate. You could tell the group that you will begin the closing prayer and then open up a time of silence so that they can also pray aloud. Make sure they know that you will close the group's prayer by leading them into an Our Father after everyone is done praying. This structure helps people feel the time is contained and not completely lacking in structure. It can also free them to pray aloud.

Below are some possible ways to introduce your group to oral extemporaneous prayer. Don't read these suggestions verbatim—put them into your own words. It's not conducive to helping people become comfortable praying aloud spontaneously if you are praying out of a book!

"The closing prayer is a great time to take the reflections we've shared, bring them to God, and ask him to help us make any inspirations a reality in our lives. God doesn't care about how well-spoken or articulate we are when we pray; we shouldn't either! We don't judge each other's prayers. Let's just pray from our hearts, knowing that God hears and cares about what we say, not how perfectly we say it. When we pray something aloud, we know that the Holy Spirit is mightily at work within us because it's the Spirit who gives us the courage to speak."

"Tonight for closing prayer, let's each voice our needs to one another; then we will take turns putting our right hand on the shoulder of the person to the right of us and praying for that person. After we each express our prayer needs, I will start by praying for Karen on my right. That means that I need to listen carefully when she tells us what she needs prayer for. We may not remember everyone's needs, so be sure to listen well to the person on your right. I'll voice my prayer needs first; then we'll go around the circle to the right. Okay? Does anyone have any questions?"

Connection to the Cross This Week

These weekly prayer and reflection exercises allow Jesus to enter more fully into the hearts of you and your small group members. If we don't give God the time that allows him to work in us, we experience far less fruit from our small group discussions. Prayer and reflection root and water the seeds that have been planted during the small group. Without these, the sun scorches the seed, and it will shrivel up and die, "since it had no root" (Mark 4:6).

Encountering Christ during the week on our own makes it possible for us to be "rooted in Christ" (cf. Colossians 2:7) and to drink deeply of the "living water" (John 4:10) that he longs to pour into our souls.

Please review the "Connection to the Cross This Week" section in advance so that you're familiar with it, and then together as a group during each meeting. This will show everyone that it is an important part of the small group. Ask for feedback each week about the how these prayer and reflection exercises are going. Don't spend too long on this topic, however, especially in the early weeks while members are still becoming comfortable together and growing more accustomed to praying on their own.

Asking about their experience with the recommended prayer or spiritual exercise will help you know who is hungry for spiritual growth and who might need more encouragement. The witness of participants' stories from their times of prayer can ignite the interest of others who are less motivated to pray.

About The Evangelical Catholic

The Evangelical Catholic (EC) equips Catholic ministries for evangelization by inspiring, training, and supporting local leaders to launch dynamic outreach. Through training events, services, and ongoing contractual relationships, the EC forms and trains Catholic pastoral staff and lay leaders for long-term evangelical efforts that can be locally sustained without ongoing site visits and regular consulting.

To accomplish this mission, we equip the lay faithful to invite the lost into the joy of life in Christ and stem the tide of Catholics leaving the Church. We form pastoral staff to make disciples, shepherd evangelistic ministries, and manage pastoral structure to make discipleship to Jesus the natural outcome within the parish or university campus ministry

Our prayer is that through the grace of the Holy Spirit, we can help make the Church's mission of evangelization accessible, natural, and fruitful for every Catholic, and that many lives will be healed and transformed by knowing Jesus within the Church.